Tomorrow   /ards
Integrity

Today's schools are subject to increasing demand and constraint; their work is more complex and fast changing than ever before; politicians and press demand quick fixes. This book paints the picture of a new integrity for our schools as they face a challenging future.

Themes addressed include:

- schools as places of learning and integrity
- the curriculum
- family, child and intercultural perspectives
- community relations
- policy and governance

Tomorrow's Schools – Towards Integrity demonstrates how a connected approach is possible and necessary if schools are to hold themselves together and play a key role in working with young people to construct a future. This is a book for everyone who thinks seriously about the future of schools.

Chris Watkins is a head of academic group at the University of London Institute of Education and course tutor to the MA in Effective Learning and the MA in School Development. **Caroline Lodge** is a lecturer in School Effectiveness and School Improvement at the University of London Institute of Education. **Ron Best** is professor and Dean of Education at the University of Surrey Roehampton.

Tomorrow's Schools –
Towards Integrity

Edited by Chris Watkins, Caroline Lodge and Ron Best

Proceeds from the sale of this book support the work of the National Association for Pastoral Care in Education

London and New York

First published 2000
by RoutledgeFalmer
11 New Fetter Lane, London EC4P 4EE

Simultaneously published in the USA and Canada
by RoutledgeFalmer
29 West 35th Street, New York, NY 10001

RoutledgeFalmer is an imprint of the Taylor & Francis Group

© 2000 Chris Watkins, Caroline Lodge and Ron Best

Typeset in Sabon by
M Rules
Printed and bound in Great Britain by
Biddles Ltd, Guildford and King's Lynn

British Library Cataloguing in Publication Data
A catalogue record for this book is available from the British
Library

Library of Congress Cataloging in Publication Data
Watkins, Chris
    Tomorrow's schools – towards integrity/Chris Watkins,
        Caroline Lodge and Ron Best. p.cm.
    Includes bibliographical references and index.
    (pbk.: alk. paper)
    1. Education–Aims and objectives–Great Britain.
    2. Educational change–Great Britain. I. Lodge, Caroline.
        II. Best, Ron, 1945- III. Title.

ISBN 0-415-23427-1 (hbk)
ISBN 0-415-23428-X (pbk)

Contents

Contributors

Ian Barr is a Director of the Scottish Consultative Council on the Curriculum. Ian has responsibility for the curriculum for children aged 3–14. His professional interests relate to holistic approaches to education, personal and social development, curriculum design, and the international dimension of education. He has published on a wide range of aspects of the curriculum in Scotland, and on international aspects.

Ron Best is Professor of Education and Dean of the Faculty of Education at the University of Surrey Roehampton. He is a founder-member and President of the National Association for Pastoral Care in Education (NAPCE). He has researched, lectured and published widely in the areas of pastoral care and personal/social/moral education and convenes the annual Roehampton conference on 'Education, Spirituality and the Whole Child'. Publications include *Pastoral Care and Personal-Social Education: Entitlement and Provision* (co-editor, Cassell, 1995) and *Education, Spirituality and the Whole Child* (Cassell, 1996). His 1996 Inaugural Lecture, 'Education and Integrity', was a stimulus for this book. Current research interests include the place of empathy in PSHE and citizenship education and the professional development and support needs of deputy headteachers.

Guy Claxton is Visiting Professor of Psychology and Education in the University of Bristol Graduate School of Education, where he directs the school-wide research initiative on 'culture and learning in organisations' (CLIO). His educational writings have addressed the practicalities of teacher education, children's learning, teacher stress (*Being a Teacher*, Cassell, 1990) and science education (*Educating the Inquiring Mind*, Harvester Wheatsheaf, 1991). His book on the 'intelligent unconscious', *Hare Brain, Tortoise Mind: Why Intelligence Increases When You Think Less* (Fourth Estate, 1997) was Anthony Storr's book of the week in the *Times Educational Supplement*, and prompted John Cleese to say: 'Just occasionally I get the feeling that someone has said something important'. His latest book is *Wise Up: The Challenge of Lifelong Learning* (Bloomsbury, 1999).

Tricia David is Professor of Early Childhood Studies at Canterbury Christ Church University College and currently head of the Centre for Educational Research. She is particularly interested in children's rights and personhood in early childhood. Since 1998, she has been leading a research project exploring early literacy in France and England. Her publications include: *Child Protection and Early Years Teachers: Coping with Child Abuse* (Open University, 1993); *Working Together for Young Children: Multi-professionalism in Action* (Routledge, 1994); *Effective Teaching in the Early Years* (Trentham Books, 1993), *Researching Early Childhood Education: European Perspectives* (Paul Chapman, 1998); *Young Children Learning* (Paul Chapman/Sage, 1999) and *Teaching Young Children* (Paul Chapman/Sage, 1999).

Neil Dawson together with Brenda McHugh created the Education Unit at the Marlborough Family Service which specialises in providing Family and Multiple Therapy for children and families where a child has shown serious emotional or behavioural difficulties at school. He is a teacher and registered family psychotherapist as well as a clinical supervisor on the MSc family therapy training at the Institute of Family Therapy in London.

Jagdish Gundara was born in Kenya and has studied in the USA, Canada and Scotland. During the 1970s he was a teacher and lecturer in London schools and colleges before becoming Head of the International Centre for Intercultural Studies at the University of London Institute of Education, where he is now Professor of Education. Since the 1980s he has worked in issues of Education for International Understanding, and he is founder and President of the International Association for Intercultural Education. He received the Bhai Vir Singh International Award from the Dalai Lama for his work in education in socially diverse societies. Publications include *European Intercultural Social Policies* (co-editor, Avebury, 2000) and *Interculturalism: Education and Inclusion* (Paul Chapman, forthcoming, 2000).

Caroline Lodge is a lecturer in School Improvement and Effectiveness at the Institute of Education, University of London. She previously served in urban comprehensive schools for twenty-five years, in Coventry and London, as history teacher, form tutor, head of department, head of year, deputy head and headteacher. She also works with schools, LEAs and careers services as a consultant, staff developer and trainer. Her research interests are learning and school improvement. She has been an active member of the National Association for Pastoral Care in Education (NAPCE) for fifteen years and was its national chair 1994–1996.

John MacBeath is Professor of Educational Leadership at the University of Cambridge. Since 1989 he has advised the Scottish Office on areas such as school evaluation, school effectiveness and improvement, and home/school relationships. He authored government guidelines including *Using Ethos Indicators in School Self-evaluation*. He was co-director of a study tracking school improvements in eighty Scottish schools, and is currently directing a national evaluation of study support. His work for the European Commission on self-evaluation has recently been published (*Self-evaluation in European Schools: a Story of Change*, Routledge, 2000) following up *Schools Must Speak For Themselves: the Case for School Self-evaluation* (Routledge, 1999). He is a member of the Government's Task Force on Standards and a member of a number of DfEE committees and working groups. In June 1997 he was awarded the OBE for services to education.

Margaret McGhie is an Assistant Director of the Scottish Consultative Council on the Curriculum. Margaret's main focus of work is Values in Education, in particular education for personal and social development. Her professional interests relate to cooperative learning, the complementary dimensions of discernment and measurement in the field of assessment, and the role of schools in promoting emotional competences in young people. She has also written extensively on a range of educational issues, both for Scottish and wider audiences.

Brenda McHugh together with Neil Dawson designed and developed the Marlborough Family Service Education Unit where she is currently joint teacher in charge. She is also a UKCP registered family psychotherapist having trained at the Institute of Family Therapy (London). She lectures on MSc and Advanced Clinical Training. She has co-authored several articles on family systems work in schools as well as a video and computer distance learning package, *Family Therapy Basics.*

John Sullivan is Head of English at a comprehensive school in South London. He has led INSET on whole-school approaches to literacy development and has been a contributor to BBC World Service education programmes.

John Tomlinson has been a Chief Education Officer, Chairman of the Schools Council, and a Professor of Education at University of Warwick Institute of Education. He has recently been President of the National Association for Pastoral Care in Education, and was Academic Secretary to the Universities Council for the Education of Teachers, 1997–2000. He is currently Vice Chairman of the General Teaching Council for England. His publications include: *Successful Schools* with Tim Brighouse (Institute for Public Policy Research, 1991); *The Control of Education,* (Cassell, 1993); and *School Co-operation: New Forms of Local Governance* with Stuart Ranson (Longman, 1994).

Chris Watkins is a senior lecturer and head of the academic group 'Assessment, Guidance and Effective Learning' at the University of London Institute of Education. Having been a teacher and a trained school counsellor, his areas of work include mentoring, tutoring, personal–social education and school behaviour – all with a central link to effective learning in classrooms and the context for teachers' learning. He has been Chair of the National Association for Pastoral Care in Education. Publications include: *Tutoring* with John Thacker (Longman, 1993); *Mentoring* with Caroline Whalley (Longman, 1993); *Pastoral Care and PSE: Entitlement and Provision* (Cassell, 1995); *Effective Learning* with others (School Improvement Network, 1996); *Learning about Learning* with others (Routledge, 2000); and *Improving School Behaviour* with Patsy Wagner (Paul Chapman, 2000).

1   From here to integrity

*Ron Best, Chris Watkins and
Caroline Lodge*

Introduction

A report in the *Times Educational Supplement* of 14 August 1998 carried a stunning photograph: against the background of red sand dunes and grey saltbush, a Kalahari Bushman stands holding a clockwork radio. The juxtaposition of the 'advanced' and the 'primitive' in this image is arresting. The addition of the headline : 'University of the air nears blast off' is sufficient to ensure the attention of anyone not already intrigued to know more. The article (it emerges) is about the World Space Corporation's decision to devote some of the digital channels of its satellites to educational programmes. The point is clearly made that the combination of space-age technology with the otherwise archaic clockwork motor may bring the information revolution even to the most remote and primitive corners of the world.

In a way, this image sums up what this book is about. The increasing sophistication and complexity of the 'global village' is manageable only if the escalating differentiation of knowledge, beliefs, values and lifestyles – personified in the contrast between the executives of World Space and the Bushmen of the Kalahari – is accompanied by an increasing integration of system parts, in this case through the dissemination of information.

This image also raises some significant questions. How will the information received on the clockwork radio affect the way of life of the listener? Whose values and whose decisions about *relevance* will determine what information the listener receives? How is s/he to be protected from abuse of the system by those who, for personal or political gain, may use it for commercial and political propaganda?

What the clockwork radio gives out will have been discussed, composed, screened, shaped, trialled, edited, refined, sequenced and enhanced before it is broadcast. This may, of course, result in sophisticated and artful presentations of knowledge which the listener would otherwise be denied and which may be advantageous to him in many ways. But it may also include a hidden – or not so hidden – 'curriculum' of ethnocentricity, religious dogma and political ideology. It may also (who knows?) contain some subliminal advertising to prepare for the dumping of consumables and other commodities of the 'advanced' world on new and unsuspecting markets.

In the latter years of the twentieth century some came perilously close to forgetting that there is more to education than the transmission of information. The idea that ICT (Information and Communications Technology) can enrich teaching, expedite learning and liberate some learners who find the more traditional media of the classroom demotivating is impossible to dispute. But our experience suggests that a preoccupation with the technology *per se* can distract both teacher and pupil from critical reflection, debate and shared exploration which education (rather than instruction, training or indoctrination – Peters 1967) entails. It is part and parcel of the ethics of education, that the intellectual independence of the learner is respected and that it is the development of the learner – and not some ulterior motive or instrumental purpose – which provides its rationale.

Not all of those who receive information courtesy of the technology and good offices of the World Space Corporation will be well placed to query, question, discuss or seek clarification or elaboration of specific points, nor to critique or collaborate with the transmitters in seeking better understandings of the information presented. Nor will many of them – especially those typified by the Bushman – be given opportunities to compose, edit and transmit their own understandings to others. In short, they will receive information in ways which are the exact opposite of those which characterise the good classroom! The Bushman may receive information but the clockwork radio is unlikely, in itself, to contribute much to his *education*.

Education is also a determining factor in how well the listener copes with the information received. In so far as one is an 'educated person', one is more or less able to discriminate, assimilate and discard information according to its intrinsic or instrumental value. It may be that the culture of the Kalahari provides its own defence against the shadow side of the information revolution, but we surely know enough of the impact of colonialism in the eighteenth and nineteenth (and, indeed, the twentieth) centuries to be wary on this score. Perhaps education holds the key. To mix our metaphors, perhaps education is the glue which will hold cultures together in a world of increasing diversity and interdependence, but we can hardly expect the institutions of education themselves to be untouched by technology, and it is clear that they are not. Nor will any aspect of our lives be unaffected by the rapid changes that are going on around us. What will become of individuals, groups and institutions in a future characterised by something as paradoxical as the reliance of the information revolution on a clockwork motor? The key concept in seeking answers to this question is, we think, that of *integrity*.

It is the purpose of this book to explore, through the developing ideas of a group of prestigious educationists, the idea of integrity and its significance for re-visioning education for the new millennium. It is necessary to begin with some analysis of the concept itself and an initial venture into the question of how and where it figures both in understanding education and considering how, through policy formulation, organisation, management and delivery of organised schooling, integrity may assume significance as a guiding principle.

Integrity and education

According to the *Shorter Oxford English Dictionary*, integrity is used in two distinct but related senses (Best 1996: 5). First, it has to do with something being whole or entire, and is etymologically rooted in the word *integer*: mathematically speaking, 'a number or quantity denoting one or more whole things or units; a whole number or undivided quantity'. Hence, integrity means 'the condition of having no part or element wanting; material wholeness, completeness, entirety'. Significantly, the concept presumes a state of wholeness which is equated with ultimate good or perfection as the alternative meanings given in the same dictionary demonstrate: 'unimpaired or uncorrupted state; original, perfect condition'. It is from this that the second main sense of the word derives: integrity as 'soundness of moral principle; the character of uncorrupted virtue; uprightness, sincerity' (Best 1996: 5).

It is the second of these meanings which is more evident in everyday usage. When we speak of someone as 'a man (or woman) of integrity', or question the integrity of an individual, we are focusing upon their morality and honesty in their dealings with others. We are affirming or challenging the moral soundness of their actions and their openness or otherwise to corruption. Implicitly or explicitly, we are commenting upon the grounds for trusting in their motives and accepting their word. In an era in which 'sleaze' has established its place in the vocabulary of politics with, it seems, all political parties seeking to discredit the claims of others to be upright, open and honest, integrity is, implicitly perhaps, more than ever the public concept which provides the benchmark against which the qualities of others and the probity of their actions are judged. Significantly, integrity is not a goal to be achieved, an aim to be striven for or an unachievable ideal: it is a presumed initial condition from which real situations have deviated. Such deviations may be thought of as fractures or, perhaps, as disintegration.

Thought of in this way, the connection between the two meanings of the word comes into focus. The presumption is that wholeness is both prior to and better than its opposite – significantly there is no precise opposite to 'wholeness' in the English language: incompleteness and partiality come close but won't quite do; disintegration describes a process or outcome of a fall from wholeness rather than its generic opposite; and the clumsy but seemingly unavoidable contrivance of 'un-wholeness' only proves the point: like the relationship of sickness to health, such concepts are departures from a presumed baseline of completeness and entirety.

That there is some ethical presumption in favour of integrity (thought of as wholeness, completeness, entirety) seems entirely reasonable since, in its more popular meaning of moral uprightness, honesty and uncorrupted goodness, integrity is clearly at home in the realms of moral reasoning and ethical practice. Perfection in form and action seems to be a common strand in both its applications, and the inference that the relationship between integrity as wholeness and integrity as moral uprightness is contingent as much as it is analytic is difficult to resist. It seems that that which is not whole is vulnerable and has little chance of withstanding corruption. Consider these popular sayings: 'In union there is strength' and 'United we stand; divided we fall' and the opposing strategy of 'divide and rule'. In Christianity (and, no doubt, in other religions too), we find the same idea: 'Every kingdom divided against itself is laid waste, and no city or house divided against itself will stand' (Matthew 12.25); 'he who is not with me is against me' (Matthew 12.30). So: if we talk of an attack on the integrity of (say) the teaching profession, we may be saying not only that the morality and uprightness of the profession and its members is being questioned but also that an attempt is being made to undermine its capacity to sustain and defend itself in the face of opposition or attempts to dominate or neutralise it.

It may also be the case that deviation from moral integrity necessarily has a de-stabilising effect on wholeness. Such is the presumption when we talk of the decadence of a society or of an individual as dissolute: to engage in immoral acts, especially of a self-indulgent kind, is considered likely to fracture the personality, cause dysfunctions in social systems or bring about the corruption of the body. While Oscar Wilde's novel *The Picture of Dorian Gray* may be about a great deal more than this (Ellman 1988), it is one of many works of art which explore the impact of less than upright conduct on the health and well-being of the actor, while in both art and history the effects of venereal disease and alcoholism on the body and mind of those who lapse from right living has long been served as 'proof' of the connection. To this day, the idea that entertainment is either 'wholesome' or 'unwholesome' seems to capture exactly the idea that moral corruption and personal or social disintegration are causally connected.

Yet if a presumption in favour of integrity as wholeness or completeness may be identified in western thought, much in our culture seems to begin with a notion of the whole as the product of a combination of constituent parts or components. It is tempting to attribute this to the fact that, since the agrarian revolution, mankind has been a species that builds. We are not alone in this, of course: birds, ants, bees and many other creatures construct nests, hives and so on from components, but the development of the processes and technologies of construction have dominated human commerce since the middle ages. The very idea that all whole entities are constructions is to be found as early as the Old Testament story of the beginning of the world: God did not make the world all at once, but bit by bit over the six days of creation. Yet this God was a God of unity and integrity: 'In the beginning was the Word and the Word was with God, and the Word was God' (John 1.1). All was of a piece, yet all creation is a construction.

What we have here is one of the most fundamental elements of our thinking, so obvious and profound that we take it as un-problematic for much of the time. When we recognise its significance we find it perplexing yet suggestive, at once unifying and differentiating, presumed in the dialectical forces of progress and growth as much as in decadence and decay: the relationship of the whole to the parts. No other idea is more pervasive in social, scientific and educational thought.

Consider the natural sciences. Nothing has preoccupied science more than the search for the single entity. In physics, the idea that there is, to be located, a basic building block of all matter led first to the concept of the atom, then to its constituent parts and, it seems, progressively to ever more tiny particles. In biology, the fascination of the single cell as the fundamental building block of all life. And so on in the search for a theoretical (and empirically verifiable) schema in which all events can ultimately be explained in terms of their causes, and all complex wholes comprehended by the relationships between constituent elements.

Consider sociology. Much of the discipline is preoccupied with the tension between social cohesion on the one hand and social differentiation and diversity on the other. For Durkheim, the problem of sustaining social solidarity in the face of the growing division of labour which accompanied industrialisation was not only an intellectual challenge to the theorist but a moral challenge to society. Significantly, the breakdown of the mechanical solidarity associated with the shared experience and common destiny of all members of pre-industrial society led to *anomie*, a condition which, for individuals, resulted in psychological dislocation, loss of identity and, *in extremis*, suicide and, for society as a whole, fragmentation, normlessness and the breakdown of the rule of law. The search for new, unifying principles led to the idea of organic solidarity, of society held together by the functional interdependence of individuals and institutions which relied upon each other precisely because they were different. For Marx and Engels, the alienation of labour was a product of technological development accompanied by the social differentiation to which it gave rise. Successive revolutions saw the increasing fragmentation of the social whole into competing classes whose exercise of economic, then political, then military power led to disaffection, exploitation and subjugation.

Consider hermeneutics, the procedures of textual exegesis and comprehension exemplified by the Frankfurt School. Rooted in the study of the Old Testament, the challenge is to come to a 'right' understanding of the text. How is this to be achieved? In a classic chicken–egg syndrome, the text as a whole may be comprehended only by the study and analysis of the constituent verses, while the meaning of each verse can be grasped only by understanding its place within the structure of the whole. From a slightly different (existentialist) starting point, Sartre (1964) arrived at a very similar conclusion: the 'right' interpretation of social/historical events required a movement back and forth between an analysis of individual praxis and an analysis of the social context of social wholes within which the actions took place. Social wholes can only be comprehended by empathy with individual actors; the motives of individual actors can only be explained by reference to the broader social and historical developments of which they are a part.

Or take social phenomenology, as represented in Berger and Luckmann's (1967) *The Social Construction of Realty*. Shared social meanings are the product of interactions between individuals, yet those individuals cannot formulate the very thoughts by which their 'because' and 'in order to' motives can be accounted other than by means of the shared meanings which comprise the symbolic universe of all meaningful social interaction. All meanings are social constructs yet the culture of an objectivated society sets the limits to what can meaningfully be thought.

In the realm of education, examples of the force and problematics of the whole-part dialectic are everywhere to be seen. The contemporary – not to say perennial – conflict between those who advocate 'whole book' and those who advocate phonics as the right approach to the teaching of reading is a glaring instance. In personal–social education, the emphasis given to the education of the 'whole person' is axiomatic and at the same time an attack upon the fragmentation of knowledge, the learner and the learning experience which follows from a preoccupation with a curriculum constructed from subject disciplines or, in Hirst's famous phrase, 'forms of knowledge'. A further manifestation is the tension between what Bernstein, as long ago as 1971, described as 'collection' and 'integrated knowledge codes' identified with the traditional subjects on the one hand and integrated studies (humanities, CDT and so on) on the other (Bernstein 1971).

In schools' attempts to cater for the needs of children with special educational needs, the debate about integration and segregation and its superficial resolution by the 1981 Education Act and the various requirements (the Code of Practice etc.) which followed in its wake is yet another example. By identifying groups of children as in any way 'special' and therefore different, and in providing learning experiences different from those of other groups, the identity of the school (or the class for that matter) as a unified whole is rendered more artificial. Perhaps for this reason, 'inclusion' rather than 'integration' is assuming popularity as the word to describe attempts at avoiding the de-unifying effects of differentiation.

Yet it remains true that the demand for integration carries in its wake the identification of those parts which are to be integrated, and in the process reproduces the conceptual distinctions between subjects and the social distinctions between learners. Similarly, the plea to educate the whole person may generate an analysis of the various 'selves' which make up that whole, and invite the design of a curriculum which consists of separate activities aimed at the development of 'separate' dimensions of the person.

Maintaining integrity

It is not our intention to argue that differentiation is the enemy of integrity. It is in the nature of social development that differentiation is inevitable. The development of individuals, organisations and whole societies is characterised by increasing differentiation but this must be accompanied by increasing integration (i.e. of the parts) if social fragmentation, *anomie* and alienation are not to result. Increasing integration without increasing differentiation leads to the narrowing of perspectives and the closing off of possibilities for that exploration and experimentation without which further growth and development are impossible.

We do argue, however, that the social, political and educational trends of recent years have lacked both integration and integrity. The emphasis upon the constituent parts – sometimes to the denial (as in Margaret Thatcher's infamous assertion that 'There is no such thing as society . . .') of the whole altogether – has been the antithesis of holism. Despite the rhetoric of the 'global village' carrying with it the notion of interdependence associated with the romanticised idyll of the rural village, not to mention Durkheim's 'mechanical solidarity' (Durkheim 1964), what has in fact developed is the post-Fordist economy of the global market. Unlike the archetypal village, characterised by common destiny, mutual support and the rhythm of the seasons, the so called global village is a market place in which the morality of the profit motive rules. What has changed is the speed at which things happen. The relative affluence and poverty of different segments of this 'village' have changed only in so far as the gap between them has grown, but now the exchange of goods and services from a position of self-interest is expedited by information and communications technology. At the risk of cynicism, exploitation now happens at the press of an e-mail key rather than the length of a telephone call, an infinitely faster process than the ocean voyage or land trek which the passage from developed to the developing world once required. The satellite and the clockwork radio are but a variation on this theme.

Two key trends in the last quarter of the twentieth century were individualisation and competition. The holistic moralities, structures, systems and processes which socialism (democratic or no) sought to establish were driven by a fundamental principle of equality between parts and the subordination of the interests of the individual to the interests of the collectivity. New Labour has recently rediscovered this idea and is using it with rhetorical force far exceeding actual commitment, in the notion of 'inclusivity' – that all individuals are to be included in (and therefore integral to) the society as a whole. But this sits oddly with competition. By definition, the parts are set against each other in competition, whether in the market place, the examination room or the board room. With the decline of communism and the fragmentation of the Soviet Union, new and reconstituted individual states rush head-long into free-market capitalism, pitted against each other and prey to the greed of those western nations (or, we should say, of the corporate capital of the western nations) only too quick to move in with investment which, inevitably, will bring an outflow of wealth to the 'donor' nations. Some good may come of this for the indigenous populations, of course, but any idea that the process of investment and the flow of profits are a feature of an inclusive 'global village' is patently absurd.

Within the UK, the marketisation of education is a particularly visible example of these trends. Local education authorities were never competitive in market terms. If there was competition, it was limited to competition for central funding in, for instance, the rate support grant, or to a sort of neighbourly rivalry with regard to the right to feel proud of one's education service in comparison with others. But LEAs have been emasculated, their integrity called into doubt and their authority over the education of their constituents eroded beyond recognition. The centralisation of control of the curriculum (from the National Curriculum Council through to the Qualifications and Curriculum Authority), the expanding brief of OFSTED (now empowered to inspect LEAs and vigorously doing so) together with the devolution of financial authority to individual schools through local management (LMS) has fragmented the provision in any area or region.

Schools once competed on the sports field and in terms of prestige in the community. The tripartite system of state secondary education from 1944 onwards may have rested on singularly narrow conceptions of human ability and aptitude, and it is possible with hindsight to see such a system as a mechanism for the inevitable social differentiation of members according to class, status and birth. But there was more than mere rhetoric in the appeal to the morality of designing a system according to the learning needs of different types of learner and the over-riding principle of parity of esteem for all three types of secondary education. Of course there was competition – the eleven-plus was all about competition – and a veritable industry of sociological research was built upon demonstrating that the competition was rigged while another industry – that of the testing movement – built itself upon the search for a fair test. But, again, this was not the kind of competition which we associate with the market.

It has taken the last two decades to establish the principles of the commodity market as those which should regulate schooling. The creation of the grant-maintained school and the customer-attractive status of city technology colleges, together with the insistence on making public the relative successes and failures of individual schools and the putative freedom of parents to send their children to the schools of their choice, have created a market (albeit distorted by the preferential resourcing of some categories of school) of a kind not seen before in education. In the last five years of the millennium, common criticisms of the most visible features of this market became clichés: that pupils are units of funding, not children; that school prospectuses resemble more closely each year a brochure for double-glazing or a corporate statement for a share float; that all grant-maintained schools spend their first grant on redeveloping their reception area to resemble that of every known insurance company.

These developments are inimical to the values of the inclusive society, for the inclusive society is – or should be – a society which conceives of itself as a whole. Parts there may be, but they are integral to that whole. Such developments would be of little consequence if they were not rooted in, and reproducing, the idea of wholes as no more than the sums of their parts. There may be nothing logically incompatible between holism and competition, but in fact the promotion of competition necessarily works against integrity because it promotes differentiation without necessarily encouraging integration.

Moreover, recent developments question the integrity of education in the second sense: that of goodness and moral uprightness. For the emphasis placed on economic efficiency, quality control, financial audit and consumer sovereignty is a distraction from the ultimately moral purpose of education. Quality control through OFSTED with its 'name, blame and shame' approach begs the question of the concept of educational success which underpins the frameworks of inspection. Linked as they are to the national curriculum programmes of study, there lurks in this process the fragmentation of knowledge, the learner and the process of learning. The emphasis on learning outcomes (so often equated with competences or technical proficiency) invites the practices of 'teaching-to-test' and 'window-dressing for OFSTED' which create the illusion of 'improving education through inspection'. Naturally enough, teachers and schools are going to do what 'works' and not what they believe is right, good or desirable.

These are attitudes which are seen as necessary for survival. After all (one might argue), at the end of the day it's our jobs that are on the line. Such an attitude seems inescapable because of the fundamental change which has taken place in public management. We believe it was Tim Brighouse, in a number of lectures and conference presentations, who first drew this change to our attention. The argument is simple: that there is a new public management which is centralist and authoritarian yet achieves its goals through a framework of apparently independent organisations compatible with democracy and objectivity. The government Agency and the QUANGO are essential parts of the mechanism by which this is achieved. In the field of education, we might mention OFSTED, the Teacher Training Agency (TTA), the Qualifications and Curriculum Authority (QCA), the Higher Education Funding Council (HEFCE) and the Quality Assurance Agency in Higher Education (QAA). What these bodies do is to articulate judgements about value (OFSTED grades, QAA ratings) with systems of rewards and punishments (student quotas, units of funding, public shaming etc.). Any school or college which fails to achieve satisfactory results is thus vulnerable both in the market where consumer preferences will be transferred to more 'successful' institutions and more directly through threats of closure, take-over, reduced funding or reduced student quotas.

The rationale which is usually advanced for this is that it is in no one's interests to have schools and colleges which are inefficient and unsuccessful and that it is in the public's (taxpayer's) interests that such quality assurance is carried out and the results made known. But what is missing from such an account is an acceptable answer to the questions: on whose concept of educational success are the assessments made and in what public domain are the criteria of acceptable performance thrashed out? What the 'new public management' does is to assert a single model of acceptable performance, demand compliance to that model, and impose these demands through a centralised system of inspection linked to funding allocations and punitive sanctions.

The integrity of those with established expertise, objectivity and a commitment to advise and support rather than to judge and condemn, has been systematically impugned in the course of the new public management revolution. In a remarkably successful smear campaign, the Tory government, aided and abetted by the popular press (represented most vividly in the pages of the *Daily Mail*), employed what Stephen Ball (1990) has termed the 'discourse of derision', in which a so-called 'educational establishment' have been systematically discredited. Specialist expertise has been derided as useless and irrelevant theory, and the technical language of pedagogy – the science of teaching – lampooned as the jargon of 'pseuds'. But such attacks were necessary to justify the replacement of established ideas and authorities with the organs of the new public management. They are to be understood in the context of the replacement of Her Majesty's Inspectorate (HMI) by OFSTED, the metamorphosis of the Schools Council into SCDC/SEAC and SCAA to become QCA, the marginalisation of other independent bodies contributing to our thinking (such as the Nuffield Foundation and the Health Education Council, not to mention Her Majesty's Inspectorate) and decimation of the advisory services of the LEAs. For these bodies all enjoyed the right to explore, experiment with, deviate from and promote the debate and critique of more and less conventional approaches to learning and teaching. The new order abhors genuine debate of fundamental educational values: this has no place in a model of public management which requires acceptance of a single concept of educational success and compliance to a single framework for the assessment of educational performance.

It is perhaps too early to say whether there has been a significant change in direction with the return of a Labour Government. True, the rhetoric of the 'inclusive society' does pay lip-service to the idea of a society in which all members are parts of the whole, but the emphasis is more to do with not being left out than with the idea that a society is (conceptually at least) a whole that is greater than the sum of its parts. 'Inclusion' may carry more positive connotations now than (say) 'integration' with its historical baggage of racial and ethnic exclusion within UK society, or within education, of the de-segregation of the 'backward, retarded and dull' traditionally thought to need special educational provision. The position of the Government on other issues, where 'zero tolerance' of deviance of any kind seems to be the watchword, is at odds with the idea of the inclusive society. The decline in local democracy is hardly to be reversed, while local education authorities remain vulnerable to OFSTED inspection and public naming. Other reforms, such as the dismantling of the assisted places scheme and the creation of new categories of school ('community', 'aided' and 'foundation') may or may not be cosmetic. Inside the school, priority must still be given to the 'basics' – the literacy and numeracy strategies and the promotion of information technology in the classroom – while the proliferation of task-groups and consultations to do with preparation for adulthood, citizenship and life in society resemble too closely the concern of the previous government with moral conformity to be convincingly presented as a break with the past.

Perhaps we should not find this so surprising. According to at least one commentator (Chitty 1998), the broad coincidence of the political strategies of Labour and Conservative Parties can be discerned at least as early as the mid-1970s. One indicator of the impact of this education policy was the famous Ruskin College speech of the then Prime Minister, James Callaghan.

The so-called 'third way' of the present government – presented as a combination of the 'realism' of the market place with the morality of socialism (now ostentatiously substituted by the concept of 'social justice') – may be seen to retrieve an important ethical dimension within politics but not at any cost to the competitive individualism of the market mentality. The tension between the whole and its parts is not resolved; if anything, it is heightened by the attempt to find a third way which accommodates, rather than transcends, the other two. Within this framework, the model of new public management is endorsed and applied daily with little sign of a real softening of the government's views on who should have the authority to determine educational priorities, curriculum content and, increasingly, pedagogic practice.

In short, while there is some evidence of a move away from competitive individualism towards a more cooperative, democratic or communitarian determination of educational policy and control of educational practice, this seems to be based more upon a pragmatic decision to ignore the deep-seated inconsistencies of the new policies than to confront them as a dialectic to be harnessed in more creative approaches. What is needed is not a facile accommodation to political expedience but a creative search for a new integrity.

Towards a new integrity in education

Where might such a search begin?

It may be helpful to return to the image with which we began: the Kalahari Bushman and the wind-up radio. We suggested that this image was arresting because it brought together, in this contraption, something new and complex (satellite technology and the information revolution) and something old and otherwise obsolete (the clockwork motor). The paradox (we implied) was in the dependence of the new and sophisticated on the old and simple. We then noted implications for the Bushman and registered the significance of education as both a necessary condition for the communication of information to be developmental and as a defence against its abuse.

Let us focus a little more on the person in the picture. He holds the radio to one side. His gaze is not on the radio, indeed, it seems not to be focused on anything. This is natural: he is, after all, listening and the other senses are at this point irrelevant. What is he thinking? Is he understanding the sounds he hears? Is he following the argument? Is he puzzling at the strange music? Is he confused by the static of a poorly tuned receiver? Is he wondering whether this has become his property? Or is he simply bemused by an artefact that makes no sense to him within his culture?

Other questions follow quickly. There are no other humans in the picture. Where is his family, his community, his tribe? Is he estranged from them? Perhaps he is a marginal Bushman, living on the edge of western civilisation, already struggling to reconcile alien cultures. There are other colonial resonances here. Perhaps the radio has taken the place of the beads and axes with which previous generations of 'explorers' and 'discoverers' traded for land with 'the natives'. His expression may be less one of concentration or puzzlement, than of anxiety in the face of the incomprehensible. It seems likely that he does not feel in any real way connected to the presenter, performer or author of the work to which he listens and we have no way of knowing how he feels about the person who gave (or sold) it to him. Does he feel disconnected, out-of-place, rootless even, in a world which, for all the apparent familiarity of the sand and saltbush, is suddenly new and alien? Can he ever feel the same about a land that is now infiltrated, courtesy of World Space Corporation and Baygen (the makers of the wind-up radio), by messages from another world?

Ask these questions and the image assumes a new significance. What is striking is the potential disruption and dislocation of this man's entire image of his life, of the world and of his place within it. We now notice the timelessness of his nakedness, of the desert, the relentless sun and shifting sands. Yet all this is threatened by what he holds in his hands, the wind-up radio with its aerial extended to receive the messages which may sound the death-knell of a way of life unchanged for a thousand years.

We can also learn from this image by examining our own reactions to it. Perhaps we expect his expression at any moment to beam with innocent delight at the wonder of this 'magic', as in the myriad Hollywood movies where everything from mirrors to muskets and gramophones to cameras have been used to 'win over the natives'. Do we feel any affinity with this man? Perhaps our expression was like this when we first encountered a tape-recorder, a PC, a video, a CD. Do we feel any connection whatever with this man, or is he as remote from us as a character in a science fiction odyssey? Perhaps our conscience is pricked by what our 'civilisation' is about to do to his culture. We may even have registered that his hair appears to be in tiny plaits, not unlike that of many members of our own communities in Britain. At some less conscious level we may even have found his creased forehead and the shape of his eyes reminiscent of those of Nelson Mandela. How do these realisations shape our reaction to this image? What does this say of our integrity? Or of his or that of his people?

There are clearly lessons here for education, for we may ask of a child in a classroom, encountering for the first time a paintbrush, a magnifying glass, a test-tube, a prayer-shawl, a spectrometer, a computer mouse, an encyclopaedia, a lump of wet clay, a tambourine or a sound-sampler: what is its significance for them? Where, in the cultures which make up our society, do such artefacts figure? How does the world look to a child who takes for granted the range and diversity of the inventions which our own life-time has witnessed? How can we make the experience that is education meaningful and integrative for each child regardless of their race, ethnicity, affluence or beliefs?

In like fashion, we may ask of our teachers, wherein lies their integrity in the age of interactive video and the 'Powerpoint' presentation?

We suggest that such questions need to be posed at a number of levels. It is not only the integrity of the individual that is important; we must think also of the integrity of the group, the class, the school, the community or neighbourhood it serves, our society and, finally, of the world which, with the Bushman of the Kalahari, we ultimately share. At each level, we need to examine not only the degree to which the whole is inclusive, to which it is recognised and celebrated as more than the sum of its parts, but also the degree to which the current structure, organisation and ethos of that whole embodies and promotes the Good. We need to probe the shadow-side of the growing complexity of the school as a social system and interrogate the degree to which schools as institutions cope effectively with the growing complexity of their catchment areas and the growing sophistication (for good or ill) of their clientele. A particular challenge for schools must be how they can maintain their fundamental values in the face of marketisation and the new public management.

The fundamental question is whether education can be a means by which social integration is maintained in harmony with growing differentiation. It is our contention that it can, but in order to do so it must encourage adaptation to new environments without sacrificing that which is enduring and timeless in the nature of education itself.

As one recent writer has argued (Ungoed-Thomas 1997), the good school is characterised by particular moral and intellectual qualities – he calls them the 'first virtues of education' – those of respect for persons, truth, justice and responsibility. These are unchanging and education would not be what it is if these qualities were not present. A moment's reflection reveals that these qualities will be observable to a greater or lesser degree in the way schools are organised and in the practices in which teachers and pupils engage. They will be pre-eminently observable in the attitudes of members to one another and in the quality of relationships which are formed between them. The morality of education lies in that care, one for another, which characterises all occasions of the growth and development of that which makes us human. Our capacity to translate care into caring practice may be a matter of social and historical circumstance – and of technological development – but the predisposition to care as a human quality is timeless.

At a more immediate level, we need to feel connected or related to others, to be accepted by others for what we are and not just for what we are able to do. Caring is made possible by membership of communities based upon trust and mutual respect, upon acceptance of one another as ultimately of equal worth. The school as a unity cannot flourish and serve its ends unless it recognises these fundamental needs and promotes and sustains those 'first virtues' without which caring is no more than an unfocused disposition.

It is not only schools which need to embody these virtues. So, to, do the teaching profession, school governing bodies, LEAs, OFSTED inspectors, responsible parents and interested citizens. Each of the following chapters explores the issues which the concept of integrity raises for an aspect or level of the education system. In each the values of care are implicit, if not explicit, and this should not surprise us. For care in the marketised society is not unlike the clockwork motor: around for a long time and thought by some to be obsolete. But care may be just what is needed to sustain, in both its senses, the integrity of education.

References

Ball, S. J. (1990) *Politics and Policy Making in Education*, London: Routledge.

Berger, P. L. and Luckmann, T. (1967) *The Social Construction of Reality*, Harmondsworth: Penguin.

Bernstein, B. (1971) 'On the classification and framing of educational knowledge' in M. F. D. Young (ed.) *Knowledge and Control*, London: Collier-Macmillan.

Best, R. (1996) *Education and Integrity*, Inaugural lecture, London: Roehampton Institute of Education.

Chitty, C. (1998) 'The "moment of 1976" revisited', *British Journal of Educational Studies*, 46(3): 318–23.

Durkheim, E. (1964) *The Division of Labour*, London: Collier Macmillan.

Ellman, R. (1988) *Oscar Wilde*, Harmondsworth: Penguin.

Peters, R. S. (ed.) (1967) *The Concept of Education*, London: Routledge and Kegan Paul.

Sartre, J-P. (1964) *The Problem of Method*, London: Methuen.

Ungoed-Thomas, J. (1997) *Vision of a School*, London: Cassell.

2 Integrity and uncertainty – why young people need doubtful teachers

Guy Claxton

Over the last five years or so I have been conducting an extensive straw poll on people's attitudes towards education. I have about 1,500 respondents now. I often give talks about learning to parents and educators, and at the beginning of each talk I offer my audience a definition of education, and then ask them a question. I define education as: 'what the "elders" of a society lay on for the young in order to prepare them to live successful, fulfilling and responsible lives in the world which they are going, as adults, to inhabit'. Then I ask people to indicate, by a show of hands, whether they think that: (a) schools as they know them do a pretty good job of equipping most young people for the future; (b) they would, if currently mooted reforms were successfully implemented; or (c) we are a long way from offering young people a good education, in this broad, generic sense. My informants so far include early years teachers and advisers, primary heads and deputies, secondary heads and whole-school staff teams, PGCE students, parents, governors and members of the inspection and advisory services. The results are clear. Out of my 1,500-odd replies, I have so far had no votes for option (a), a total of thirteen for (b), and the rest for (c) (with very few abstentions). I sometimes ask a supplementary question of those who have voted for (c): do you have a reasonably clear idea of what needs to happen, or are you really not at all sure how we are to deliver such an education? Nearly all opt for the latter.

I conclude that the vast majority of people who work in, or care about, education feel in their bones that it is failing, in this basic sense, to equip young people to deal with the rigours and complexities of the real, uncertain world. They believe that current reforms of curriculum and assessment procedures, however hotly promoted or contested, are tinkerings that do not get to the heart of the problem. And they don't know what to do about it. This is the reality. Yet most of these people, and most of the rest of us, most of the time, seem to act as if we believed that schools were more-or-less OK, and that changes to the way literacy is taught, or to the 'A'-level syllabuses, were worth fighting over. The dissonance between 'IT ISN'T NEARLY GOOD ENOUGH' and 'WE DON'T KNOW WHAT TO DO' is so intense that it has to be buried under a big pile of busy-work.

In its everyday use, the word 'integrity' means both 'integrated' and 'moral'. A person who has, or acts with, integrity is one who 'does the right thing' or 'speaks the truth', in terms of their personal morality, especially when it is hard to do so. Their deeper, inner sense of what is true and what is right permeates their awareness, their speech and their actions. They are, to use Carl Rogers' famous synonym, 'congruent' (Rogers 1961). Or, as the *Oxford English Dictionary* puts it, they have 'the character of uncorrupted virtue' – uncorrupted by shallower or more expedient motivations, perhaps. To have integrity is to (dare to) manifest what you know (or believe), in your heart of hearts, to be true and right. In these terms, my survey starkly reveals that the world of education, at the moment, profoundly lacks integrity. The overwhelming majority of people feel deeply dissatisfied and confused, yet their words and actions continually belie these uncomfortable perceptions and emotions. Thus we are led to the strange conclusion that the institution in our culture that is most explicitly concerned with learning seems fundamentally unable to admit the depth and extent of its own need to learn.[1]

Learning starts from the joint acknowledgement of inadequacy and ignorance. 'It's not working, and we don't (immediately) know how to fix it.' There is no other place for learning to start. An effective learner, or learning culture, is one that is not afraid to admit this perception, and which also possesses some confidence in its ability to grow in understanding and expertise, so that perplexity is transformed into mastery. Jean Piaget once defined intelligence as 'knowing what to do when you don't know what to do'. Good learners are intelligent in this sense. They are *resilient*, capable of tolerating the emotional discomfort of operating under uncertainty. They are *resourceful*, equipped with a practical repertoire of tools and tactics for finding things out. And they are *reflective*, able to maintain an accurate overview of their own learning progress and priorities, and to manage their learning accordingly (Claxton 1999). To have integrity, therefore, both the individuals and the institutions of education would need to be better equipped than they are now with these 'three Rs'. Somehow the people who deliver education, and who are in charge of deciding what it will be like in the future, seem unwilling or unable to bring much in the way of resilience, resourcefulness and reflection to bear on their own professional world.

This lack of integrity means, therefore, that the pace and depth of educational innovation are retarded and diminished. Change does not happen as much as it could – and perhaps should. But there is more than a social or political argument here. There is a complementarity, an integrity in the sense of interconnection, between the need for education itself to be more involved in its own learning, and the needs of its customers for a more fulfilling preparation for an uncertain future. For it can be strongly argued that it is precisely the same mental trinity of resilience, resourcefulness and reflection which young people themselves need if they are to be educated for the 'real world' in the sense in which I defined education at the beginning of this chapter. Young people will need, above all, to be 'good learners': curious, confident and capable explorers of a fast-changing culture. Their teachers need to be good learners, as they re-think the nature of education. And it is predominantly by being around adults who are themselves good learners – who have the courage to make their own uncertainties visible, and to model intelligent engagement with hard problems – that young people pick up the capabilities and dispositions that they will need. That, in essence, is the argument of this chapter.

Feeling adrift in 'the age of uncertainty'

If parents and teachers strongly suspect that schools do not give students the start in life which they need, there is evidence that young people themselves are acutely aware of the same lack. The Industrial Society survey *Speaking Up, Speaking Out* (1997) reports the results of questionnaires and interviews with 3,500 11–25-year-olds across Britain, designed to uncover their views about the future. The conclusion makes depressing reading.

> Most [young people] fear that their world will generally become more challenging, and some have a bleak view of future opportunities and trends . . . Their lives are riddled with insecurity . . . Insecurity becomes an integral part of growing up . . . Schools are seen as failing to equip young people with the ability to learn for life rather than for exams.
>
> (p. 265)

One 19-year-old woman spoke for many when she said: 'A lot of the time at school they teach you the knowledge, but they never teach you how to learn.' This pervasive feeling of insecurity – of being faced with uncertainties and difficulties that they do not feel equipped to deal with – manifests in specific fears, for example about employability and redundancy, and physical safety (75 per cent of all the young people surveyed are afraid of being attacked). Many interviewees share the pessimistic view of their own ability to learn expressed by a 17-year-old from Devon, who said: 'The thing I'm scared of is say I got laid off, I've got nothing, nothing to help me get another job. I've got no other skill.' And young people readily admit that this sense of insecurity fuels all kinds of escapism: into a romantic view of relationships and even parenthood; into the essential importance of friendship and socialising; and even into the use of drugs and extreme physical activity to shake off, temporarily, the feeling of oppression that dogs so many of them. 'If you're insecure anyway or you've got a problem . . . and somebody comes along and says, you know, I've got something, what do you want . . . it's just a way of escaping it'.

Young people rightly perceive that the break-up of the old certainties and traditions of a job for life, stable community and a singular, consensual morality creates both exciting freedoms and onerous responsibilities. We are rapidly moving, as Harvard educationist Robert Kegan (1994) puts it, from 'automatic' to 'stick-shift' cultures, in which, instead of the culture guiding and determining the major channels of development for the majority of people, they can make it up for themselves. The title of Kegan's book, *In Over Our Heads: The Mental Demands of Modern Life*, sums up what these young people feel. The conditions of modern life demand a kind of mentality that many of them do not feel they possess, and they feel let down by an education system that has peppered them with arcane activities while apparently neglecting this glaring need. They wanted to be helped to become good 'choosers' and good learners, and they didn't get it. As their teachers were busy denying their own uncertainty about the worth and appropriateness of the education they were delivering, so too they seemed blind to the wider and deeper real-life learning challenges with which their students were already being faced.

When people do not 'know what to do when they don't know what to do', and when they are frightened of the feelings and conditions of learning – the risks attendant upon sustained engagement with complex uncertainties – they feel stressed and become defensive. Stress is often defined as a perceived imbalance between demands and resources which can be resolved in one of three ways. You can make efforts to reduce the demands. You can attempt to manage the ensuing emotionality through the familiar processes of denial, projection, displacement, rationalisation and so on (e.g. Salzberger-Wittenberg *et al.* 1983). And you can invest in increasing your resources. The first is, if you like, the 'action' or political option. The second is the psychological option. And the third is the educational option. Whilst all have their place, it seems as if the education system as a whole, despite the valiant efforts of some individuals and sub-cultures within it, has shied away from the challenge of attempting to increase young people's resilience, resourcefulness and reflectivity in the face of real-world uncertainty.

Teaching to learn: blind alleys and productive paths

Attempts to train people directly in the generic skills and dispositions of learning have, by and large, been disappointing. Coaching in study skills and learning strategies is often well-received (perhaps in part because it make a welcome change from normal content-focused regimes that are perceived as dull and difficult), but its effects are equally often short-lived, and fail to show transfer to other situations, or to come to mind spontaneously when required (Nisbet and Shucksmith 1986, Nickerson *et al.* 1995). In addition, there is evidence that direct, formal attempts to teach the tools of learning, even if they are partially successful, may unwittingly undermine the development of the disposition to make use of that tool. As Katz (1999) has pointed out, there is a world of difference between being able to read, and being a reader. Marcon (1995) has shown that trying to teach the skills of literacy too early results in a long-term decrement in the disposition to read. Just so, we might be sceptical of both the efficacy and the wisdom of too-earnest and too-direct an attempt to train the development of learning.

Instead, it appears that positive learning capabilities and dispositions develop together most effectively within what can best be described as a 'learning culture': a milieu which in its very *modus operandi* is designed to encourage both the expression and the development of inquisitive, learning-oriented abilities and attitudes. Teachers around the world are beginning to make impressive progress towards creating these cultures in classrooms – when the explicit requirements of curriculum and assessment, and the implicit dictates of school ethos and tradition, permit it. So-called 'ordinary' students seem to show an enthusiasm for engaging with substantial learning challenges, and for flexing and stretching their 'learning muscles', when the conditions allow. In Australia, Cosgrove (1995) has shown how small groups of such students enthusiastically boot-strap their own learning when faced with a scientific problem which they have the time and encouragement to get their teeth into.

They relished the opportunity to reason through to a conclusion, and to take part in extended debates in which there was strong reliance on the evidence provided by tests they had planned and carried out themselves, to discriminate amongst the possibilities they proposed. After a time, these students showed the capacity to take some control of their learning. They gave up asking the teacher for all the answers, confident that they could work problems out for themselves.

(p. 306)

The class teacher himself observed, with some surprise:

The thing that impresses me is how far they have come . . . They are automatically sieving out what does not fit with what they have seen. And they are only accepting and hanging on to what they see . . . And only ideas which might be right are accepted and tossed around. They are not interested in me telling them anymore. They have moved right away from 'What's the right answer?' . . . What they really want is for me to say 'That sounds like a good idea', or 'What if this was tried?' And they go off and think.

(p. 307)

Karen Hume, a teacher working with socio-linguist Gordon Wells in Toronto, has shown how even apparent resistance to participative, inquiry-based teaching can be used to hook students' interest, and help them develop their learning (see Wells 2000). Working with a group of young adolescents in a new school, she included, as was her normal practice, a good deal of exploratory and discussion-based teaching. After a week or two, she asked the class for feedback on her methods. The students were enthusiastic – with the exception of Andrew, who 'absolutely *hated*' all the talking. Karen suggested that he might like to take a deeper look at why discussion evoked such different responses in people. With a group of classmates, Andrew undertook a systematic investigation of how discussions proceeded, what made some of them productive, and why some seemed to run into the ground. The group analysed transcripts, even taping and reflecting upon their own discussions. Together with the teacher, they produced a report summarising their data and their conclusions. Karen Hume comments on the ways of working which they developed in terms strikingly similar to Cosgrove's.

My students are behaving as apprentice researchers. They make connections to their experiences and to each other in support of their developing theories. They identify themes and patterns across data. They demonstrate an ability to reflect on and critique data, even words they themselves have said ('I disagreed with myself a couple of times!', said Eddie), when evidence fails to support their earlier claims. Perhaps most important, there is considerable talk in all meetings of the strategies we have used in our analysis. This is beneficial not only because it makes apparent that the kids are choosing and using strategies but because, in making the strategy explicit, it is open to use and modification by others.

(Wells 2000)

I have been working with teachers in a primary school in the South of England to develop ways of increasing children's 'learning power'. In a Year 6 class, 10-year-olds have collectively produced their own list of 'good learning behaviours' (a phrase which the class teacher, Beverley Ball, has borrowed from Baird and Northfield's (1992) account of their Project for the Enhancement of Effective Learning (PEEL). Posters of these self-generated hints about 'what to do when you don't know what to do' are pinned up on the classroom walls, reminding the students of their own resourcefulness when they get stuck. This list is, of course, being continually up-dated as students discover for themselves more and more facets of 'good learning'. A class of younger children in the same school are using their penchant for fantasy as a way of improving their stickability in the face of difficulty or frustration. The class teacher has introduced an 'imaginary friend' – 'Lucy' – to whom the children have been invited to attribute their own ideas about what makes a 'good learner'. When a child is having difficulty with their learning, and is on the verge of getting upset, the teacher may ask gently 'What would Lucy do?', or 'Would you like to be Lucy now?', and sometimes this is sufficient to lend the child extra reserves of resilience – reserves which, next time, they may tap spontaneously for themselves.

The integrated learning curriculum

Such changes to the classroom climate seem to share a number of common characteristics. Often the problems which students are working on are genuinely difficult ones. It seems to help if they are ones to which the teacher does not have a ready-made answer. (When you know that the teacher knows what the answer to your 'inquiry' ought to be – as in the typical school science experiment – learning feels like a simulation rather than a genuine voyage of discovery.) It is better if the students have had at least a bit of a hand in generating the problems themselves. It helps if there is time for the inquiry to be sustained and cumulative. It helps if it is carried out, at least part of the time, in a group of peers, all of whom are interested in the problem and willing to pool ideas and strategies. It helps, too, as Ann Brown (1997) and others have shown, if the classroom as a whole is constituted as a collection of such small 'research teams' working on related problems, each of which is required to give regular summaries of their progress to the others.

Examples of isolated classroom practices such as these – and there are many – are still only the first step, though, on the road towards a 'learning curriculum' that has real integrity. For there are at least three different senses in which such practices become more powerful if they are integrated. First they need to be integrated 'vertically' into a more coherent and explicit sense of how young people's learning ability increases over time. School curricula are based on a (largely intuitive) sense of what young people are ready to study at different ages, but the fascination with the transmission and testing of specific bodies of subject-matter has led to a widespread neglect of the more general 'growth of mind' that underlies the mastery of specific competencies.[2] If education is to aim, not just in rhetoric but in reality, to help young people develop 'a mind to learn' – an inquisitive mentality that will serve them well in the real world of adulthood – it has to take a cumulative, developmental view of learning capabilities and dispositions.

Second, the curriculum needs to be integrated 'horizontally', across the different subjects and specialisms. Different kinds of learning topics and materials pose different kinds of learning challenges, and therefore afford opportunities to develop different compartments of the mental tool-kit. From this point of view, what differentiates the writing of poetry from the study of biology is not so much their contents as the ways of knowing and learning that each calls for, and therefore serves to exercise and develop. Both of them, for example, afford the opportunity to practise meticulous observation, maybe even of the same object. Ted Hughes has been much praised as a poet for his detailed depictions of animals – a horse, a fox, a baby pike – and in his radio talks to children (Hughes 1967) he enjoins them to base their poetic efforts, too, on the same patient observation. ('Keep your eyes, your ears, your nose, your taste, your touch, your whole being on the thing you are turning into words . . . See it and live it. Turn yourself into it).' The poet's *modus operandi* is here not so very different from the working methods of the naturalist. But what use they then make of these observations: that is very different in the two disciplines. And both the empathic and imaginative use of the artist, and the deductive and analytical use of the scientist, have their place in the full portfolio of learning modes which the lifelong learner may be glad of. (The whole power of the 'scientific method' is of course destroyed by a rushed curriculum which cannot wait for students to see, and think about what they do see, but has them write down what they should have seen, and move hurriedly on.) The work of looking at the school curriculum as a whole, in terms of the developing repertoire of learning skills that are distributed across the different subjects, and trying to extract a coherent programme and rationale from that diversity, has hardly begun. Approaches such as Gardner's (1991) 'multiple intelligences' make a start, but only that.

Teaching for transfer: learning skills 'to go'

But integration within the school curriculum is not enough, if we are looking to the wider aim of preparing young people to live a learning life. The capabilities and dispositions they develop within school have to transfer to contexts and problems that occur out-of-school. And as we saw earlier, the problems of teaching for such transfer are not trivial. If 'learning skills' are transmitted as an abstract body of knowledge or a content-free training programme, they remain disembodied and do not offer any practical purchase on real-life, real-time predicaments. On the other hand, if learning strategies are taught in the context of a single kind of subject-matter, they remain tied to the contents, contexts and tasks in which and for which they were learnt, and do not spontaneously transfer to other situations to which they might potentially be applicable.

To make sure that learning skills are both practically embedded and maximally portable, Halpern (1998) has shown that for effective transfer to occur, four essential elements are needed. First, there must obviously be opportunities to learn and develop the requisite skills. For example, if one wishes to help students develop the capacity for 'critical thinking', then its constituent skills, such as recognising and discounting the sloppy use of language, analysing the validity of arguments and unearthing unstated assumptions, have to be explicitly described and deliberately practised using realistic examples. However, if only a narrow range of examples are used, then the skills developed tend to stay tied to that domain, so the second element of teaching for transfer has to be practice at recognising when a particular skill is appropriate. Sometimes it is possible to describe the appropriate domain explicitly; sometimes it has to be discovered through experience; sometimes both. Halpern has found that, where possible, a mixture of both explicit and experiential learning is most effective. Third, one has to make sure not only that students are developing the skills but that they are developing the disposition to use them. To think well, one must be not only able, but ready and willing to do so. Halpern has found that false assumptions about the nature, and sometimes the difficulty, of thinking may undermine the willingness and the determination to think to the best of one's ability, so she holds regular discussions with her students that are designed to dispel these unhelpful beliefs. It has been shown by Schommer (1990), for instance, that some students believe that 'learning is quick or not at all', or that 'thinking is either easy or useless', and that those who hold these beliefs are less likely to persist in the face of difficulty (because, if these beliefs were true, there would be no point in doing so). Thus explaining to students that thinking and learning are sometimes hard and that persistence can pay off, encourages the development of the disposition to persist.

Finally, for the likelihood of transfer to be maximised, it is vital to give students opportunities and encouragement to develop their 'metacognitive awareness' of their own thinking and learning abilities, which they can use to guide their mental processes for themselves. People who understand their strengths and weaknesses as learners and are able to monitor their own minds so that they can take strategic control and manage their own learning effectively, are also more likely to recognise the applicability of one type of mental skill in the context of a different-looking domain. The ability to be reflective about oneself, and one's own mental and emotional processes, is developed in a climate in which the teacher or other more experienced learners are able to model such 'learning aloud', and encourage students to practise it for themselves. Just as student teachers need to be able to watch their mentors being 'reflective practitioners', so too do younger students in school. Learning how to externalise and articulate one's own learning process probably deserves more attention in courses of teacher education than it currently gets.

Being an example: parents and teachers as agents of enculturation

The most influential element of the students' learning milieu is not the tasks and materials they are given but the teachers they are exposed to. Through both their use of language and their non-verbal demeanour, teachers signal to students the values and beliefs they hold about learning and knowing, as well as about the learning capabilities and 'proper' interests and aspirations of groups (defined, for example, by gender, ethnicity or socio-economic background), and individuals. What teachers notice, and conversely what they ignore, sends clear messages to their students about what is valued within the classroom culture and what is not. Their casual comments and asides, what makes them laugh, how and when they feign anger (or genuinely 'lose it'), what they are patient and impatient about, and so on: all these intended and unintended communications are inviting students into a cultural view of what is to be seen as creative, what is routine, what is naughty, what is stupid, what is unkind. And teachers' comments, both formal and informal, on students' learning likewise inducts them into an 'epistemic' world-view: a set of assumptions about how learning proceeds, the best methods of learning, the relative values of easy success and intelligent persistence, who generates knowledge and who is mandated to evaluate it, how and by whom student learning is to be assessed, and so on.

A familiar illustration of the subtle ways in which parents' and teachers' language influences young people's development as learners is revealed by the kinds of explanation that elders offer for students' successes, failures and difficulties. Frome and Eccles (1998) have shown that parents typically account for their sons' and daughters' success, failure and difficulty in different subjects in different ways. A daughter's success in mathematics, for example, is often attributed to hard work, while her failure is taken to reflect lack of ability. Conversely, a son's mathematical achievement is greeted as a sign of talent or aptitude, while his lack of success is attributed to laziness. Such attributional commentaries, Frome and Eccles show, translate directly into youngsters' attitudes towards learning. If you are told, effectively, that your difficulties reflect a lack of ability, there is little you can do about it. You might as well withdraw or mess about. If you have been led to believe, on the other hand, that failure is due to a lack of effort, then improved performance through increased effort is a real possibility. To summarise a complex story in a simplistic causal sequence: the wider learning-related beliefs of the society install themselves in the 'implicit theories' and assumptions of teachers, where they dissolve into the micro-structure of their verbal interactions and non-verbal demeanour. Students are sensitive to these behaviours, especially when they are young, and the beliefs and values that inform those behaviours are thus transferred and installed in the minds of the next generation, shaping the kinds of learning capabilities and dispositions which they develop, and changing, for good or ill, what learning challenges they feel able to engage with, and how.

The elders do not just convey beliefs about the learning capabilities of specific individuals and groups; children's development as learners is channelled by more impersonal, generic beliefs about learning and the mind that are held (often unconsciously) by their parents and teachers. Dweck (1999), for instance, has shown that children's learning is directly affected by the way in which their elders conceptualise 'ability' itself. She contrasts two views of ability: one as a relatively fixed, ubiquitous reservoir of general-purpose mental capacity which effectively sets a ceiling on achievement; and the other as a learnable set of learning tools and attitudes. Through the informal processes of cultural apprenticeship described above, either of these views may be transferred to the young learner (largely unwittingly). It turns out that learners who have been infected with the former 'fixed' view of ability tend strongly to have a much more brittle kind of engagement with learning than those who have been brought up with the 'expandable' view.

Adults induct young people into the views of their culture through their actions as well as their words. As we have seen, their patterns of attention and evaluative reaction to what others are doing convey beliefs about what is important and worthwhile. But adults also teach their culture through the actions they choose to involve themselves in, and the ways they respond to the vicissitudes of their own experience. Young people learn a tremendous amount about their culture just from watching and 'eavesdropping' on their elders as they go about their business. (We even now know that the disposition to learn through observation and imitation is evolutionarily hard-wired. There are so-called 'mirror neurons' in the cerebral neocortex that respond both to the visual experience of a certain kind of hand movement, for example, and the production of that same movement (Rizzolatti *et al.* 1999).)

Thus the models that adults provide of learning, and of what it means to be a learner, are likely to be powerful stimuli for the development of young people's own capabilities and dispositions. It is a fair bet (though this would be hard to quantify in any objective sense) that prolonged exposure to a relatively small sample of adults – parents, teachers and media figures, pre-eminently – all of whom are, willy-nilly, modelling a set of attitudes towards and habits of learning and knowing, is a more effective determinant of young people's development as learners than any particular regime of explicit instruction or exhortation. Thus it becomes very important to know what kinds of capabilities and dispositions are being modelled, as teachers, for example, go about their business of imparting particular bodies of knowledge and expertise.

Back to integrity: daring to model 'confident uncertainty'

When Albert Einstein was once asked for his views on education, he reportedly replied: 'The only rational method of educating is to be an example.' And he added: 'If you can't help it, be a warning example.' On the view I have developed here, it would be a tragedy if 'being a warning example' – an example of fearfulness and narrow-mindedness, of clinging to the known in the face of important challenges and unavoidable uncertainties – was the best that (some) teachers were able to muster. Yet, if the discussion with which this chapter started is anywhere near the mark, schools up and down the land are full of teachers who are pretending to be more certain than they are – at least about the deep-down value of the education which they are doing their best to deliver. Not only are educators deeply confused about what they are doing; their attempts to manage this confusion by denying it are actually depriving young people of the learning role models which they urgently need, if they are to pick up the positive learning capabilities and dispositions which the 'real world' is demanding of them.

In the field of learning, as in any other, the elders teach their integrity, or their lack of it. Just as people can often tell when a friend is in a state of dissonance – they are more angry or upset than they are letting on, even perhaps to themselves – so it may well be that young people in school not only are being deprived of learning role models, but are internalising instead models of incongruity and role strain. It may well be that one of the causes of the high levels of teacher stress is this (often unacknowledged) inner dissonance, and that the attempt to manage this becomes increasingly costly in 'emotional energy'. It may also be that, as students watch, day after day, performances of tension and denial, of controlling and dogmatic attempts to deny confusion and insecurity, so that is what they are learning. They too are learning to meet uncertainty by becoming tight, tense and dogmatic.

Scary though it may be, the only hope of developing an education that is equal to the times may be for teachers to dare to stand up *en masse* and say 'It isn't good enough' and 'We don't know what to do'. Out of that may come, before it is too late, a debate of the requisite degree of depth and urgency about what education for the 'age of uncertainty' needs to look like; and also, if we can carry it into our classrooms and seminars, the beginnings of the necessary revolution itself. Teaching is no longer about knowing; it is about demonstrating how to maintain intelligent engagement with complicated predicaments, how not to freeze up in the face of confusion and frustration. In beginning to engage more vigorously and passionately with their collective uncertainties, teachers (and other adult role models too) may also begin to reveal to young people what it truly means to be a lifelong learner.

Notes

1 Ivan Illich (1973), once defined an 'institution' as 'an organization designed to frustrate its declared goal'. As transportation systems get more sophisticated they deliver slower journey times. Hospitals are the places where people are most likely to get sick. And so on.
2 The developmental stages offered by Jean Piaget – sensorimotor, pre-operational, concrete operational, formal operational – are too crude and sweeping to be helpful in this context.

References

Baird, J. R. and Northfield, J. R. (eds) (1992) *Learning from the PEEL Experience*, Melbourne: Monash University Press.

Brown, A. (1997) 'Transforming schools into communities of thinking and learning about serious matters', *American Psychologist*, 52: 399–413.

Claxton, G. L. (1999) *Wise Up: The Challenge of Lifelong Learning*, London: Bloomsbury.

Cosgrove, M. (1995) 'A study of science-in-the-making as students generate an analogy for electricity', *International Journal of Science Education*, 17: 295–310.

Dweck, C. S. (1999) *Self-Theories: Their Role in Motivation, Personality and Development*, Philadelphia PA: Psychology Press.

Frome, P. and Eccles, J. (1998) 'Parents' influence on children's achievement-related perceptions', *Journal of Personality and Social Psychology*, 74: 435–52.

Gardner, H. (1991) *The Unschooled Mind: How Children Think and How Schools Should Teach*, New York: Basic Books.

Halpern, D. (1998) 'Teaching critical thinking for transfer across domains', *American Psychologist*, 53: 449–55.

Hughes, T. (1967) *Poetry in the Making*, London: Faber and Faber.

Illich, I. (1973) *Deschooling Society*, Harmondsworth: Penguin Education.

Industrial Society (1997) *Speaking Up, Speaking Out: The 2020 Vision Research Report*, London: The Industrial Society.

Katz, L. (1999) *Another Look at What Young Children should be Learning*,

ERIC Digest, University of Illinois: ERIC Clearinghouse on Elementary and Early Childhood Education.

Kegan, R. (1994) *In Over Our Heads: The Mental Demands of Modern Life*, Cambridge MA: Harvard University Press.

Marcon, R. A. (1995) 'Fourth grade slump: the cause and cure', *Principal*, 74: 17–20.

Nickerson, R., Perkins, D. and Smith, E. (eds.) (1995) *The Teaching of Thinking*, Hillsdale NJ: Lawrence Erlbaum.

Nisbet, J. and Shucksmith, J. (1986) *Learning Strategies*, London: Routledge and Kegan Paul.

Rizzolatti, G., Fadiga, L., Fogassi, L. and Gallese, V. (1999) 'Resonance behaviors and mirror neurons', *Archives of Italian Biology*, 137: 85–100.

Rogers, C. R. (1961) *On Becoming a Person*, London: Constable.

Salzberger-Wittenberg, I., Henry, G. and Osborne, E. (1983) *The Emotional Experience of Teaching and Learning*, London: Routledge and Kegan Paul.

Schommer, M. (1990) 'Effects of belief about the nature of knowledge on comprehension', *Journal of Educational Psychology*, 82: 498–504.

Wells, G. (2000) 'Inquiry as an orientation for learning, teaching and teacher education' in G. Wells and G. L. Claxton (eds.), *Learning for Life in the 21st Century: a Socio-cultural Approach to the Future of Education*, Oxford: Blackwell.

3 The child

Tricia David

Integrity

The idea of a new integrity for education is discussed in Chapter 1 and here I will consider the child's integrity. First, the child's integrity could be considered to mean 'wholeness' so that for education purposes we ask ourselves questions about the ways in which we promote learning in all areas of human development – physical, social, emotional, cognitive, aesthetic and spiritual. 'Wholeness' could also be said to be involved in the way in which each of us 'makes sense' of the different roles (one might almost say different personae) we take on in different situations and with the different people to whom we relate. Second, integrity can mean 'uprightness' and in this respect we would need to examine the extent to which education promotes children's moral development and fosters action born of a sense of being 'true to oneself'. In considering both aspects of integrity in relation to children, it seems important to recognise the central role played by 'identity'. In his study of young children's learning, Pollard (1996) suggests that the factors influencing the sense of identity in each child he tracked are found first and foremost in the home and in the years from birth to five. He concludes that the children's relationships with others inform their emerging sense of identity. Integrity in both senses demands the ability to make connections, within oneself and in relating to other people and one's world.

Born to be social: the ecology of childhood

So do children come into this world in some way equipped with integrity, or does society need to ensure uprightness is taught and that all children's areas of development are fostered? Recent research suggests that they are in fact 'programmed' to make sense of the situation in which they find themselves and to communicate with other human beings and that they will live 'up or down' to societal and family expectations, that they will try to please the adults around them in order to be valued, loved and accepted.[1] In other words, human infants are born to be social and to act in ways which will give them a 'place' in their respective communities.

It is through the growing impact of contact with very different cultural beliefs about young children that greater recognition for the social nature of young children's learning and the cultural context in which that learning is accomplished has been realised. Also, the tremendous ability of even very young babies to 'make sense' of that cultural context has only recently been acknowledged in academic work. During the first half of the twentieth century the methods of child study adopted by psychologists tended to be laboratory-based and their adoption of natural science approaches meant they rejected information reported by the children's parents or carers as too subjective. The result was that for many years babies and young children were not accorded the powers psychologists now acknowledge and a number of researchers have questioned the ways in which developmental psychology, because of its underlying assumptions and methods, failed to access those powers (e.g. Deloache and Brown 1987; Singer 1992).

We now know that from babyhood, human beings have dispositions to learn different things. They are not simply bundles of biological urges slowly being transformed, as they pass through universal pre-set stages of development, only to become fully formed humans as adults. On the contrary, babies are active learners about their worlds and the people who inhabit them right from the moment of birth – perhaps even before that.

Research reported by the Carnegie Corporation (1994) has demonstrated that a lack of stimulation in the very early years can result in actual damage to the brain, ultimately preventing optimal achievement. We also have evidence that brain development during early childhood is not only crucially dependent upon positive environmental and experiential factors for its later optimal functioning, it may also become relatively 'hard-wired' during this period (Diamond and Hopson 1998).[2]

At the same time, according to constructionist theory, early childhood is a period of relative plasticity (e.g. Bogin, 1998). This plasticity allows different cultural and social groups to interpret children's biological make-up in different ways, overlaying it with particular constructions of how children are expected to 'be', what childhood is 'for' and, thus, what might constitute appropriate forms of education (Tobin *et al.* 1989; Nunes 1994). For example, some contend that the view of children as 'adults in waiting' represents a particularly Minority World approach to childhood, learning and the curriculum (Hazareesingh *et al.* 1989), an approach which limits expectations, and in turn limits achievements.

The recently developed Sociology of Childhood (see Prout and James, 1997), an area of study which draws on many disciplines,[3] has highlighted the question of why different societies construct childhood in particular ways and why certain childhoods are assigned to particular children. The team which carried out the international study *Childhood as a Social Phenomenon* (Qvortrup *et al.* 1994) under the auspices of the European Centre for Social Policies and Research concluded that 'childhood is marginalised (or excluded) in a society in which adulthood is thought of as being of paramount importance' (*ibid.* 21). Work in the field of sociology of childhood challenges certain western/northern child development theories because of the assumptions on which the theories have been based and the ways in which findings have been generalised, despite the research from which the theory has been derived having been conducted in a very specific cultural context. Morss (1996) argues that this type of developmentalism may be hegemonic, seeking to impose one particular model of childhood and upbringing on different societies and subcultural groups with the collusion of developmental psychologists.

However, children themselves are not like passive lumps of clay being shaped into whatever contortions a society may choose, far from it. They are active participants in the process – but children are born to be social, so they will want to be accepted by and to please those around them and so this 'shaping' involves the children themselves. The important point to remember is that although the plasticity means that children can be shaped by their communities' expectations of them, the shaping process involves certain potential abilities or dispositions being reinforced or enhanced and others allowed to 'die off'. The problem is that once an ability has been allowed to die off it will be more difficult to revive it in later life, because of the effect of the concomitant early 'hard-wiring'.

The kinds of childhood we have been constructing through adherence to a somewhat fixed, staged developmental model, usually based on Piagetian theory, may have inadvertently paid insufficient attention to the interaction between the biologically based capabilities with which babies come ready equipped and the importance of the richness – or otherwise – of their early cultural experiences. In other words, we should perhaps change our assumptions and thinking from the derivation of Piaget's ideas which argues that 'development creates windows of opportunity for learning to happen' and begin to think more along the more Vygotskian lines of 'learning promotes development' and it happens through meaningful and emotionally-laden social interactions.

So first, if we fail to recognise the potential and plasticity of young children's development, we may limit their achievements unless we can decide which aspects of our cultures and which abilities will be the most valuable in the future, to the individual children themselves and to their societies.

Second, awareness that all learning takes place in a social context where cultural ideas and attitudes are transmitted, should lead us to be more caring and careful about each child's 'ecological niche'[4] and the kinds of 'hard-wiring' being promoted. In fact, the education and upbringing we decide on for our children, both its content and its teaching approaches, may have crucial long-term consequences for our society. Without ignoring the intra-personal factors with which each child is born, we have to decide what kind of people we want our children to be and to become and foster that development through the provision of appropriate interactions and experiences, building on the child's own dispositions and the foundations laid in the home.

Whole children? Emotional and spiritual dimensions of development as aspects of integrity

Affective aspects of learning, children's emotional involvement with those around them, are now acknowledged as an important issue, since they have a major impact on the depth and quality of the experience (Roberts 1995). 'Emotional intelligence' has become a high priority (Goleman 1996), having been neglected by our education system in the past.

In a similar way to the neglect of emotional learning, there has been a neglect of the spiritual aspects of children's education, again an aspect which relates to a human core of being. Here too community and meaningful social interactions are seen as crucial by Newby, who puts forward a view of spiritual development as the development of personal identity: 'spiritual development is progress from ill-being to well-being . . . responsible, and with the interests of the community at large in mind' (Newby 1998: 97).

We are slowly realising our responsibility to the earth and our need to live in harmony with nature rather than seeking domination. Perhaps as a nation, we may have to undergo an equivalent realisation with respect to babies and young children and in particular our responsibility to enable their emotional and spiritual development. For it is through our emotional and spiritual engagement with others that we truly relate and are able to empathise.

The foundations of robust emotional health and the ability to relate well to others seem to be laid in the very early years of childhood and point to the need for a curriculum in which the child has greater autonomy and is encouraged to be creative and imaginative, supported by 'knowledgeable others'. Research from the USA in particular indicates that ultimately nations save money if they address this issue (Sylva 1998).[5] Attention needs to be paid to curriculum areas which foster emotional and spiritual as well as social, physical, aesthetic, moral and cognitive development. Limiting the main focus of education in schools to formally taught literacy and numeracy has important consequences. Even if the strategies succeed, do we want a nation of people who are literate and numerate at the expense of their emotional health? Surely we require attention to literacy and numeracy as well as the other areas of learning and to 'whole people'?

Unfortunately, a recent Council of Europe project on culture, creativity and the young (Robinson 1997) has found that because governments are anxious about the interplay between the economy and social and cultural change, the dominant emphasis of the school curriculum on maths, science and language is forcing the arts and humanities to the periphery and certainly in England there is a downward pressure on early educators to follow this trend. What seems especially depressing about such a finding is that it is happening at a time when research on right-left brain function is demonstrating the importance of the areas of the brain *not* used for or developed by the narrow core of favoured curriculum subjects (for example, Claxton 1997).

Howard Gardner (1983) has drawn attention to the way in which western education systems have traditionally fostered only a limited number of 'intelligences'. In the light of Robinson's research, this appears to be a trend which is increasing rather than decreasing. At the same time we are becoming more knowledgeable about early plasticity and about the early 'hard-wiring' of the brain, as discussed above. Putting all this evidence together, we might now begin to challenge the wisdom of the limited view of curriculum prioritising literacy and numeracy which has been imposed on schools and nurseries in England, since it does not have the breadth to promote development in both sides of the brain, nor 'whole people'.

Growing and changing

As we begin the twenty-first century, the urge to reflect upon past achievements and failures seems an imperative. We need to ask ourselves: what do we want our children to be and to become? What do we hope for them? Who has the right and the responsibility to take decisions about the shaping of subsequent generations and to what extent are the children and young people involved in those decisions? And if, together, we can formulate some ideas about the future society we would like, have we any ideas about how this can be achieved?

The people of Reggio Emilia in a region of Northern Italy designed their early childhood education system, in the aftermath of fascism, on the perspective of the child, with the explicit intention not of teaching children to obey but to 'nurture and maintain a vision of children who can think and act for themselves' (Dahlberg 1995: 8). As well as the responsibilities expected of teachers here in the UK, their teachers are required to engage in public activism about education issues and conduct systematic research to further curriculum planning, teacher development and professional dissemination (Edwards *et al.* 1998). Teachers in the Reggio nurseries hold an

> image of the child as rich, strong and competent . . . unique individuals with rights rather than simply needs . . . It is our belief that all knowledge emerges in the process of self and social construction. Children . . . do not just passively endure their experience, but also become active agents in their own socialisation and knowledge building.
>
> (Rinaldi, in Edwards *et al.* 1998, 114–15)

Above all the nurseries of Reggio Emilia are learning communities where everyone is seen as growing and changing. The staff are constantly learning, documenting the children's learning and reflecting upon their observations, being helped by special advisory teachers during their one session per week of continuing professional development, often advised to read research material from a range of disciplines. The whole community is learning, for parents, politicians and nursery staff meet to discuss what goes on in their nurseries and the ideas informing policy and practice. Their discussions include topics such as 'What is a child?' as well as what they want for their children.

The investment in the nurseries is of paramount importance to the community and each setting is beautifully housed and equipped, with an atelier (workshop) for an artist in residence, each of whom works alongside children and staff. The children learn through child-directed play and relevant thematic experiences. There is no prescribed curriculum. Reggio's founder, Loris Malaguzzi has stated the belief that:

> our schools do not have, nor have they had, a planned curriculum . . . If the school for young children has to be preparatory and provide continuity with the elementary school, then we as educators are already prisoners of a model that ends up as a funnel . . . Its purpose is to narrow down what is big into what is small.
> (Edwards *et al.* 1998: 87–88)

Above all, it is this view that children can be 'rich, strong and competent', given appropriate facilities and staff attitudes and approaches, which marks out the nurseries of Reggio Emilia as promoting children's integrity. For there children develop the ability to make decisions for themselves, based on their own assessments of a situation, as well as the wholeness which comes from being 'stretched' in all areas of their development and learning.

Although we cannot know for certain what their lives in the twenty-first century will be like, we need to ask ourselves what, if anything, we in England hold as a vision of education which will equip our children for lifelong learning in a post-industrial, 'high-tech' world, where environmental, health and other global concerns are likely to be even more acute than they are today (David *et al.* 1992).

Perhaps part of such a vision involves educationists in being observers of children, problematising childhood, exploring the different childhoods being experienced by children from different contexts and backgrounds, and reflecting on the ways in which gender, race, class and special need are part of those differing constructions. By listening to and watching children in settings familiar to them, we can find out their interests and help them not only to co-construct their world but also to co-construct the people they themselves are.

Our beliefs about childhood and the place of children in society impact upon policy and practice. Like the teachers of Reggio Emilia, we can promote debate to help our communities recognise children as *people* (rather than as either 'adults in waiting' or objects, the possessions of their parents – see David 1996), people with active minds, eager and programmed to learn, and able to influence their own childhoods. Such debates will also lead us to reflect on decisions about curriculum because they too reflect the values and ideology underpinning society. Tomlinson states: 'When a society makes an educational policy it makes an image of itself and of its vision of the future' (Tomlinson 1986: 1).

Curriculum, community and connectedness

What then do we see in our current government's policies? There are fears that literacy and numeracy (extremely important skills though these are particularly for those who do not acquire them easily) are being overemphasised at the expense of children's other powers and are being taught more in relation to the economy and employment than as life skills. Politicians constantly remind us that these skills are necessary so that we are able to compete in the world market. Yet surely our vision of the future should be one aiming for world cooperation, mutual respect and care – for each other and for the environment? Literacy and numeracy alone cannot promote the kind of whole and upright people who will live in and fashion such a world, nor can these curriculum areas alone promote the sense of connectedness and community which will be needed to sustain such a world.

At the beginning of this chapter, I suggested that integrity and identity are dependent upon the ability to make connections – within oneself, relating to others, relating to one's world. Integrity and identity involve independence and interdependence. The ability to think and act independently is crucial to integrity and to identity – it was a major factor in the decision of the people of Reggio Emilia to create a system of nursery provision which would provide a foundation for later life intended to produce human beings who would not unthinkingly obey orders, to obviate the possibility of another fascist regime. The Reggio philosophy informs our thinking about integrity in the moral sense, since it means having the ability to make decisions one can live with even in the face of opposition. Further, since the interdependence of everyone in each community and nursery is again a key aspect of their thinking, the idea of integrity as the ability to 'make connections' is also informed by Reggio's approaches. The children help the adults learn, they are not seen as 'adults in waiting', or as 'empty vessels' to be filled up with static knowledge by their educators. The model of childhood adopted in these now world-famous nurseries is one which epitomises integrity in both senses. Perhaps most importantly, even the youngest children in Reggio Emilia are seen as 'rich and powerful' in their creativity, their ability to influence their world and their efforts to 'make sense' of their unique experiences.

Communities' civic covenant with children

The UN Convention on the Rights of the Child (United Nations 1989) has become a key piece of legislation for us in the field of early childhood education. The Convention has been criticised on a number of counts, for example, that it divides children off from other sections of the population; and that it is the Minority World's view of how childhood should be, rather than allowing communities to define childhood and children's rights for themselves.

However, O'Neill (1994) argues that each generation inherits a 'civic covenant' which includes a moral responsibility for the generations which follow, implying the need to value children – and presumably to act as role models with integrity. He claims that the power of the global market must be restrained, that capitalism has always been dependent upon moral and political restraints to keep it from destroying itself. In other words, if we do not elect governments which pay attention to the needs of the weakest (or rather least powerful) members and we allow individualism free rein, ignoring social responsibility, we risk a total collapse of society. We cannot dis-embed the economy from society; it too must have integrity.

In developing our own vision of an education system for a society with integrity, which in its turn promotes the integrity of pupils, parents, policy-makers, teachers and communities, we might fruitfully reflect on the words of the poet Kahlil Gibran, celebrating the idea that each child and each generation develops new ideas because of their creativity and unique experiences. We can provide children with the means to develop integrity but then we must trust them to think and act for themselves:

> You may give them your love but not your thoughts,
> For they have their own thoughts . . .
> For life goes not backwards nor tarries with yesterday.
> You are the bows from which your children as living arrows are-
>   sent forth.
>   (Gibran 1926, in the 1994 edition: 20)

Notes

1 See, for example, work by Bruner and Haste (1987); Trevarthen (1992; 1993). In the early years of developmental psychology it was thought that human babies must undergo a set sequence of development so that they pass through all the stages of development of the species. Additionally, the relative importance of inherited characteristics and those learned through one's upbringing were debated and researched in a kind of 'nature versus nurture'

battle. Now psychobiologists and neurophysiologists are affirming the complementarity – not the duality either/or nature, of human physical make-up and experience. Jean François Lambert suggests the earlier, futile debate raged as a result of an overadherence to the Rationalist stance that 'reason is quite independent from sensory experience' (Lambert 1996: 23). Evidence from research by the Post-Piagetians in the UK and Australia (for example, Donaldson 1978), by Bruner in the USA and the UK (1977, 1990), together with Vygotsky's (1978) ideas from Russia and most recently Trevarthen's (1992) in Britain, has challenged the limited, Western/Northern view of child development as fixed to a particular pattern in every sense.

2 Lambert argues that babies under a year old have a finer ability than that of adults to distinguish between sounds ('until they are one year old, American babies can recognise a Hindi phonemic contrast, non-existent in English, that older children and adults are unable to recognise': Lambert 1996: 27); within the first few months babies have a coherent idea of their mother tongue. Of course, babies and young children cannot be left to fend for themselves but it seems they are not predisposed by biology to be powerless and helpless. Given an appropriate context, they are powerful members of their group or family. Lambert explains much of this in terms of new ideas about neural development: in babies there are far more nervous connections than in the adult. For example, a human baby under one year old has the necessary neural 'equipment' to learn any language in the world but, presumably because the use of first/home language focuses on those brain connections related to this, from the first birthday the capacity to speak other languages dies away (i.e. the nervous connections related to other 'foreign' sounds 'die off'). Similarly, in a bird such as the marsh sparrow the songs of the babies comprise four or five times as many syllables as those of the adult birds. While we can appreciate the practical reasons for such losses, the very idea turns upside-down assumptions about babies as incapable and incomplete biological bundles and adults as complete – the pinnacle of development.

3 It is possible that the sociology of childhood owes its origins to the psychologist William Kessen, who argued that communities shape the young and that childhood as we know it is a 'cultural invention'. His groundbreaking paper, 'The American child and other cultural inventions' (Kessen 1979) was written after he participated in a delegation which visited educational settings for children in China in the mid-1970s (Kessen 1975).

4 For further information about Bronfenbrenner's ecological theory of human development, which brings together ideas from sociology and developmental psychology, see, for example, Bronfenbrenner (1979; 1992) and Bronfenbrenner and Morris (1998).

5 The adults who experienced the American High/Scope curriculum as young children have now been monitored for over two decades and their lives and achievements compared with peers who did not experience early childhood education through this project. In summary, the High/Scope graduates have been more successful academically and socially and now new evidence shows that they are less likely to have emotional illnesses than their non-High/Scope counterparts. Thus, it is claimed that the early investment in a curriculum based on child-directed, adult-supported learning repays the economy handsomely.

References

Bogin, B. (1998) 'Evolutionary and biological aspects of childhood' in C. Panter-Brick (ed.) *Biosocial Perspectives on Children*, Cambridge: Cambridge University Press.

Bradshaw, J. (1990) *Child Poverty and Deprivation in the UK*, London: National Children's Bureau.

Bronfenbrenner, U. (1979) *The Ecology of Human Development*, Cambridge MA: Cambridge University Press.

Bronfenbrenner, U. (1992) 'Ecological systems theory' in R. Vasta (ed.) *Six Theories of Child Development*, London: Jessica Kingsley.

Bronfenbrenner, U. and Morris, P. A. (1998) 'The ecology of developmental processes' in W. Damon (ed.) *The Handbook of Child Psychology. Volume 1: Theoretical Models of Human Development*, New York: John Wiley.

Bruner, J. (1977) *The Process of Instruction*, Cambridge MA: Harvard University Press.

Bruner, J. (1990) *Acts of Meaning*, Cambridge MA: Harvard University Press.

Bruner, J. and Haste, H. (eds.) (1987) *Making Sense*, London: Methuen.

Carnegie Corporation (1994) *Starting Points: Meeting the Needs of Our Youngest Children*, New York: Carnegie Corporation.

Claxton, G. (1997) *Hare Brain Tortoise Mind*, London: Fourth Estate.

Dahlberg, G. (1995) 'Everything is a Beginning and Everything is Dangerous', Paper given in honour of Loris Malaguzzi, International Seminar, University of Milan October.

David, T., Curtis, A. and Siraj-Blatchford, I. (1992) *Effective Teaching in the Early Years*, Stoke-on-Trent: Trentham Books.

David, T. (1996) 'British babies: people or possessions?' in D. Hayes (ed.) *Debating Education: Issues for the Millennium*, Canterbury: Canterbury Christ Church College.

Deloache, J. S. and Brown, A. L. (1987) 'The early emergence of planning skills in children' in J. Bruner and H. Haste (eds) *Making Sense*, London: Cassell.

DES (1978) *Report of the Committee of Enquiry into the Education of Handicapped Children and Young People. (Warnock Report)*, London: HMSO.

Diamond, M. and Hopson, J. (1998) *Magic Trees of the Mind*, London: Penguin/Dutton.

Donaldson, M. (1978) *Children's Minds*, Glasgow: Fontana.

Edwards, C., Gandini, L. and Forman, G. (1998) *The Hundred Languages of Children*, London: Ablex.

Gardner, H. (1983) *Frames of Mind: The Theory of Multiple Intelligences*, New York: Basic Books.

Gibran, K. (1926) *The Prophet*, London: William Heinemann.

Goleman, D. (1996) *Emotional Intelligence*, London: Bloomsbury.

Hazareesingh, S., Simms, K. and Anderson, P. (1989) *Educating the Whole Child – A Holistic Approach to Education in the Early Years*, London: Building Blocks/Save the Children.

Kessen, W. (ed.) (1975) *Childhood in China*, New Haven: Yale University Press.

Kessen, W. (1979) 'The American child and other cultural inventions', *American Psychologist*, 34(10): 815–20.

Lambert, J. F. (1996) 'Des règles et du jeu', Paper presented at the European Seminar of OMEP, UNESCO Paris, 24–27 October.

Morss, J. (1996) *Growing Critical: Alternatives to Developmental Psychology*, London: Routledge.

Newby, M. (1998) 'Towards a secular concept of spiritual maturity' in R. Best (ed.) *Education, Spirituality and the Whole Child*, London: Cassell.

Nunes, T. (1994) 'The relationship between childhood and society', *Van Leer Foundation Newsletter*, Spring, 16–17.

O'Neill, J. (1994) *The Missing Child in Liberal Theory*, London: University of Toronto Press.

Pollard, A., with Filer, A. (1996) *The Social World of Children's Learning*, London: Cassell.

Prout, A. and James, A. (1997) *Constructing and Reconstructing Childhood* (second edition), London: Falmer.

Qvortrup, J. (1990) 'A voice for children in statistical and social accounting' in A. James and A. Prout (eds) *Constructing and Reconstructing Childhood*, London: Falmer.

Qvortrup, J., Bardy, M., Sgritta, G. and Wintersberger, H. (1994) *Childhood Matters*, Aldershot: Avebury.

Roberts, R. (1995) *Self-esteem and Successful Early Learning*, London: Hodder and Stoughton.

Robinson, K. (1997) 'Great expectations of raising standards', *Times Educational Supplement*, 29 August, No. 4235: 15.

Singer, E. (1992) *Child Development and Daycare*, London: Routledge.

Sylva, K. (1998) 'Too much too soon?' Keynote address, Islington Early Years Conference, 9 July.

Sylwander, L. (1996) 'Why we need an Ombudsman for children' in Council of Europe, *The Child as Citizen*, Strasbourg: Council of Europe.

Tobin, D., Wu, D. and Davidson, D. (1989) *Preschool in Three Cultures: Japan, China and the United States*, London: Yale University Press.

Tomlinson, J. R. G. (1986) *Public Education, Public Good*, University of Warwick Inaugural Lecture, 2 June.

Trevarthen, C. (1992) 'An infant's motives for speaking and thinking in the culture' in A. H. Wold (ed.) *The Dialogical Alternative*, Oxford: Oxford University Press.

Trevarthen, C. (1993) 'The functions of emotions in early infant communication and development' in J. Nadel and L. Camaiori (eds) *New Perspectives on Early Communicative Development*, London: Routledge.

United Nations (1989) *The Convention on the Rights of the Child*, New York: United Nations.

Vygotsky, L. (1978) *Mind in Society*, Cambridge MA: Harvard University Press.

4   Curriculum for the future

Margaret McGhie and Ian Barr

This chapter argues that, despite convincing analyses of the changes taking place in the world and the kinds of capability young people need to deal effectively with that world, schools and the curriculum have in fact changed very little in the last hundred years. The importance of basic skills is accepted, but these need to be fostered in a learning environment where connections between and among the components of the curriculum are regularly and consistently made, and where the objective must be secure understanding of key ideas rather than the accretion of disconnected 'knowledge'.

The chapter goes on to make the case that curriculum content is to an extent arbitrary, but that there are bigger design considerations that need to be applied to whatever content is deemed appropriate. Certain experiences should be an on-going entitlement for all students, core skills should equip young people for a world characterised by continuing and sometimes discontinuous change, and certain dispositions need to be fostered if we are to live in a caring and responsible society. From such a set of curriculum criteria, we would be more likely to derive a set of learning experiences that would foster well-being in an uncertain world.

'Plus ça change . . .'

President Dwight Eisenhower, talking of the need for change, once said, *'Things are more like they are today than they ever have been.'* The same might well be said of education. In some respects education has changed. There is now an almost universal demand for access to extended education. In Britain much more is now expected of schools and they are central to the lives of virtually all young people from age 4, to age 18. There is, rightly, an ever-increasing emphasis on the concept of 'life-long learning', with school days being regarded as only

one highly important set of experiences in an on-going educational journey.
In many respects, however, little has changed. In terms of the curriculum, the timetable, the environment in which learning takes place, and the techniques of teaching, the nature of the school experience of those who were at school in the early decades of the twentieth century is almost identical to that of education in the 1960s. These, in turn, are fairly indistinguishable from the experiences of young people currently in schools. Teaching is still generally understood as largely about the transmission of ideas, concepts and facts.

> Teaching techniques have certainly become more sophisticated, but verbal exposition, questioning, the printed word, paper and pencil remain the essentials. The fundamental logistical question in planning the school system remains 'How many little people should you put in a box with a big person?
>
> (Bloomer 1999)

Pre-eminence is still given to the literacy and numeracy that formed the basis of the education of working class children in the early days of mass education. With few amendments and with an audience that is now gender equal, the curriculum is still that defined by the '*professionalisation*' of knowledge (Whitehead 1948), that restrictive practice whereby groups secured the power of certain domains of knowledge which became their exclusive property and thus a means of access to the professions. Despite wide recognition of the importance of life skills, higher status is still accorded to the 'academic' as opposed to the 'vocational'. Judgements are still made about young people, based to a very great extent on their ability to recall information or demonstrate decontextualised skills – they are led to believe their futures literally depend on it. And the secondary school day is still divided into neat segments and with young people organised into age-defined groups.

It almost seems as if we had persuaded ourselves that at some time in the past we found an everlasting and perfect blueprint, bar some minor tinkering, for school education, regardless of the nature of the world in which it takes place. That the school curriculum and its organisation are enduring is certain. While this might be a fine characteristic for national monuments, ancient buildings or even the monarchy, is it one that should be ascribed to a responsive school curriculum?

New understandings of the learning process

The old model persists despite new understandings of how learning happens. Schools continue to be organised in a manner unlikely to be conducive to the ways in which people learn. We know that learning advances by connecting new knowledge with what is already known, yet the secondary school curriculum is still made up of separate components, with no real obligation to make connections among them. In addition, the knowledge base is assumed to be essentially the same for everyone, rather than differentiated by the individual accessing the information, their own particular needs and purposes. The choices people make in every other aspect of their lives are personal. They read, listen, watch, discuss, investigate to find out what they as individuals want and need to know. Individuals construct their learning to make personal meaning, yet schools continue to offer the same menu to all young people and judge their success by the extent to which they conform or not to its parameters. People learn in many different ways using different 'intelligences' (Gardner 1983), yet schools focus particularly on and value some intelligences more than others.

> When everyone must pass through the same narrow eye of the needle, those youngsters whose aptitudes are appropriate for that eye succeed, and those whose aptitudes lie elsewhere have little or no opportunity for those aptitudes to be expressed or realised. If you want to create educational diversity you need to diversify the forms so that all students in the school can have a place to shine. Where someone is able to shine depends on the kind of game that's being played. If the only game in town is basketball (I'm 5' 7"), then I'm out of luck.
>
> (Eisner 1994: 6)

In short, the curriculum continues to be based on beliefs which no longer accord with the processes of learning as they have come to be understood, and have little to do with the lives that young people actually lead.

There is some awareness that all is not well. We are told that we are failing to compete in international markets, that standards of literacy and numeracy are slipping, that a civil society is an aspiration rather than a reality, and that we live in a materialist world. And yet, despite this catalogue of shortcomings we still hold fast to practices which have manifestly failed. We struggle to make education better by the curious device of giving out more of that which hasn't worked. If some cannot read, what better remedy than to give them more reading; if numeracy is a problem, add an hour of sums to their day. This is not to suggest that young people need not know the basics. Far from it, they need to know how to read and to write, otherwise a whole universe is closed to them. They need to know how to count, otherwise they cannot easily make their way through the day. Young people also need to know how to do these things to make sense of the world as a whole, not simply to make sense of schoolwork. Nevertheless, a pre-occupation with literacy, with numeracy, with the recall of information as a prime indicator of success, and with the cognitive, fails to recognise that young people need to and will develop as rich complex human beings. They lead lives and have minds that are many-sided; they have thoughts and ideas and feel strongly about a whole range of subjects. School must pay careful attention to this truth.

> A child may hardly know how to read or write, but he has keen eyes and ears and an already well-developed sense of self – of his obligations and responsibilities, of his likely difficulties, his possible future achievements, and most of all his particular task as one who comes from a particular race and place and time.
>
> (Coles 1996: 354)

Children from the very beginning make sense of the world in a holistic way. They do not understand it as separate bits, but as part of their joined-up daily lives. Yet much of formal education presents them with learning experiences that are fragmentary and unconnected, in contrast to their out-of-school learning. Experiences in school do not stand alone. Young people need the help to make connections between what they learn in school and their experiences elsewhere in their increasingly complex world. They also need to be helped towards a sense of belonging and personal achievement in the many different dimensions of the world around them. As Carl Rogers said as long ago as 1975, it is time to come to terms with the notion that:

> learning might be significant to young people because it bears upon what they think about their girlfriends, what they think about politics, what they think about the whole world, rather than letting them continue to suppose that it is irrelevant to their lives as a whole because it was done in a classroom, because there was a context label on it, and it was only education anyway.
>
> (Rogers and Bateson 1975)

It would seem reasonable, given the nature of the world we inhabit, to conclude that there is an urgent need for a new model of curriculum for schools. A new model cannot take as its template the old structures – it is the old structures that are the problem. Far from educating young people for the future, schools are in many ways educating young people for a world that is past, using structures that are at odds with the frameworks of the world outside school. School education, although well intentioned, risks increasing irrelevance to life now and as we imagine it might be.

The structure and content of the curriculum

A central purpose of school education is the initiation of young people into the knowledge, skills and values of society. Usually in the West there are three aims that derive from that purpose: socialisation of the young, the teaching of certain forms of knowledge, and a realisation of personal uniqueness. The socialisation objective is firmly focused on preparing children for the 'realities' of life as they will lead it. The curriculum that derives from this aim is negotiable, open to change and 'relevant' to 'real life'. The 'forms of knowledge' objective aims for the initiation of the young into Matthew Arnold's 'best that has been thought and said in the world'. The third objective, the realisation of personal uniqueness, is intent on developing the 'whole' person' and the individual's full potential.

The problems of each of these aims are well rehearsed: the socialisation aim leads to an over-attention on current matters of concern, the 'bodies of knowledge' model is too fixed on the notion of objective 'truth', and the personal development model fails to recognise sufficiently the extent to which learning is socially constructed and built on intellectual skills. The Platonic 'bodies of knowledge' approach, which is most explicit in a subject-based curriculum, is most firmly embedded in the public mind and in public discourse as what constitutes a curriculum. It seems a fixture in the system. 'We are so used to mangled curricula, however, that their fundamental incoherences are accepted as necessary "tensions" produced by the competition of "stakeholders".' (Egan 1997: 206). Interdisciplinary strategies, cross-curricular themes and integrated approaches have made valiant efforts to address the issue of curricular connectivity, but have often fallen into the traps of becoming hopelessly unfocused, or of attempting to ape the subject model by constructing their own hierarchies and taxonomies. The personal fulfilment model can founder in an over-enthusiasm for personal and social development devoid of intellectual rigour. The tension between these three equally important aspects will always be an on-going difficulty for schooling.

But regardless of curriculum structure, the intention must always be the same: to enable young people to grow and develop as individuals in social settings who have understanding of certain key fields of intellectual endeavour, and who can contribute to the society that they are part of. In order to influence and construct futures, it is imperative that there are connections among the various components of the curriculum however it is described. We live in a relational society that requires human interaction across ever-changing contexts, and in a knowledge society that requires collaborative learning and a focus on meaning-making and knowledge-building rather than simply information processing.

Subjects

In talking of school, Michael Oakeshott describes it as a special place of learning whose distinctive feature is:

> firstly that those who occupy it are recognised and recognise them-selves pre-eminently as learners, although they may be much else besides. Secondly in it learning is a declared engagement to learn something in particular.
>
> (Oakeshott 1989: 24)

What constitutes the 'something in particular' is, of course, the con-stant challenge and that debate will always be dominated by the political needs of the moment, by societal values and beliefs, by subject interests and by firmly held and often conflicting views of what it means to be educated. Currently curriculum guidelines provide specific content detail, often formed into attainment targets. It seems to be important to know about the Vikings, the capital cities of Europe, or the novels of Thomas Hardy, although it is rarely clear why. As with any canon, it can be replaced by another equally valid and intellectu-ally respectable list. Furthermore, the arbitrariness of the choices is made more transparent by the fact that in a world increasingly awash with easily accessible, un-mediated and rapidly out-of-date facts and information on every topic under the sun, many young people can find out more in an evening than their teacher could tell them in a life-time. A transmission model of teaching with the teacher personified as the fount of all knowledge is hardly tenable.

What is needed is a curriculum structure that is connecting, but which does not damage the distinctiveness of whatever content is included. Subjects and courses need to be organised to ensure they help young people make sense of the world.

> I don't think disciplines should be loved for their own sake; they ought to be seen as the best way to answer questions that human beings are interested in. I see the purpose of education as helping people to understand the best answers that cultures and societies have come up with to basic questions . . . So in the end we form our own personal answers to these questions, which will be based to a significant extent on how other people have approached them, and will at the same time allow us to make our own syntheses.
>
> (Gardner 1999)

Perhaps there are certain ideas and knowledge which, experience suggests, help accomplish personal sense-making and social integration. It might be helpful to think of these in terms of domains rather than isolated subjects. Making sense of the world cannot proceed very effectively without some acquaintance with the 'big ideas' in language, in technology, in science, in the world of the arts and in the spiritual and moral dimension.

Many young people leave school with certificates congratulating them on their achievements but without having much, if any, grasp or secure personal understanding of the distinctive broad ideas and concepts which have contributed to the sum of human understanding at the heart of each 'subject'. It is not clear what use students are to make of the Mathematics or History they have learned unless they have understood it and made connections with their own world view. Understanding is the *personal* construction of knowledge and the objective of the curriculum must be to make knowledge meaningful to students.

Knowledge and understanding

Just as we use 'mangled' curriculum structures we confuse and camouflage the important distinctions between 'knowledge and understanding'. In the desire to define content, facts and information become confused with knowledge, and knowledge with understanding. Conceptually, understanding is difficult to pin down. Some writers relate it to use. Gardner, for example, proposes that:

> An understanding is the capacity to use knowledge or skills in

ways in which you have not been explicitly trained, but is appropriate for a particular kind of problem or project that you are involved in.

(Gardner 1996)

Perkins and Blythe similarly describe understanding as:

> being able to carry out a variety of actions or 'performances' that show one's grasp of a topic and at the same time advance it . . . understanding is a matter of being able to do a variety of thought-demanding things with a topic – like explaining, finding evidence and examples, generalising, analogising and representing the topic in a new way. . . . It is being able to take knowledge and use it in new ways.
>
> (Perkins and Blythe 1994: 6)

In this view, learning requires teachers to present the students with 'through-lines' that 'help students see the purposes that underlie their daily work, make connections among various topics and assignments and reach their own developing understandings' (Blythe *et al.* 1998: 41).

Perhaps Entwistle and Entwistle get closest with a description given by an undergraduate student. While taking a cognitive perspective, the interwoven emotional agenda is also clear.

> Understanding? It's the interconnection of a lot of disparate things – the feeling that you understand how the whole thing is connected up – you can make sense of it internally. You're making lots of connections which then make sense and it's logical. It's as though one's mind had finally locked in to the pattern. Concepts seem to fit together in a meaningful way, when before the connections did not seem clear, or appropriate or complete. If you don't understand it's just everything floating about and you can't quite get everything into place – like jigsaw pieces you know, suddenly connect and you can see the whole picture. But there is always the feeling that you can add more: that it doesn't necessarily mean that you didn't understand it; just that you only understood it up to a point. There is always more to be added. But if you really understand something and what the idea behind it is, you can't not understand it afterwards – you can't de-understand it. And you know you have understood something when you can construct an argument from scratch – when you can explain it so that you feel satisfied with the explanation, when you

can discuss a topic with someone and explain and clarify your thought if the other person doesn't see what you mean.

(Entwistle and Entwistle 1992)

The theme of connections re-emerges here, as in the statement: 'Understanding is, of course, just a question of relating something to something else' (Pramling 1990: 19).

Big ideas

Teaching for understanding is a complex challenge. All the more reason to avoid unhelpful complications. The need is for clear curriculum specification of the 'big ideas' that need to be revisited over time in order to consolidate understanding in any particular subject or course. Whatever the content, the objective must be to encourage the development of key understandings. While it is important to know how grammar works, this is not an end in itself but an integral part of the bigger picture of knowing about language – how it gives form to and influences our thoughts, allows them to be communicated, and is instrumental in developing human relationships. Art and music may teach young people skills, but should also help them to understand how the arts convey thoughts, feelings and emotions by means of symbol systems other than words. History may describe events in the past, but the big ideas are understanding of cause and effect, chronology, and of how societies come to be the way they are.

The subject curriculum with its canon of 'knowledge' and skills can lead to a neat and tidy-minded determination of attainment. It does not provide the basis for demonstrating secure understanding of key ideas. Nevertheless, moves to reduce the knowledge base of any syllabus or course are resisted for fear that any such reduction will damage levels of attainment. If the erroneous idea that more *knowledge* equates with greater attainment could be dispelled and replaced with the more secure idea that better *understanding* equates with greater attainment then curriculum specification could be much simplified, teaching liberated and effective learning enhanced. Attainment, far from deteriorating, would rise as students built on their prior understandings and motivations.

Essential experiences

We are not making a case for a curriculum without subjects. Rather, we suggest that all subjects, whatever they might be, should contribute distinctive educational experiences. In science for example, students should experience investigative work that will encourage them to formulate their working hypotheses and develop their own strategies for testing their ideas. In social subjects they should gather evidence from a variety of sources and sift what is valuable and relevant. In creative and aesthetic subjects they should experience the excitement of expressing feelings and ideas in various media. Thinking of 'subjects' in terms of contexts to realise important experiences may also be a helpful way of deciding which should be included in a curriculum.

But there are other experiences which students must encounter in school life in order to be able to deal constructively with systemic change; to think creatively and with maturity about personal change; to understand how to effect change and how to live happily with the consequences. These are capabilities that the future will demand of them and that are best developed by means of certain essential experiences. They are essential because they help equip young people to respond with resilience, creativity and equanimity to the only thing in the future about which there is certainty – that the future will be uncertain. Essential experiences should help young people to be disposed to think, act and feel in ways that enhance both their own feelings of self-worth and their relationships with the world around them. They should encourage the growth of self-confidence, of maturity, of social responsibility and of personal well-being, and should equip young people to respond with confidence and resilience to the varied demands that life will make of them.

If young people are to be capable of facing the future with optimism and confidence they should encounter a variety of opportunities to experience:

- *Sharing responsibility*: it is essential that young people be involved in the negotiation of rights and responsibilities and experience the democratic process in action. Responding to the diverse and complex society in which we live means recognising the interconnectedness and interdependence of all our lives and the need to act with respect and responsibility towards others.
- *Working both co-operatively and independently*: it is essential that young people develop the capacity to act autonomously in the pursuit of their own needs and purposes. They should also have opportunities for team working and collaboration with others in a range of situations and tasks. In a world characterised by diversity, it is important to learn how to accept compromise in the reconciliation of different interests and to develop a shared sense of purpose. It is also important to recognise when compromise is not appropriate.

- *A sense of achievement*: it is essential that young people know what it means to succeed. Knowing that there are very many ways to do well and that these are recognised and celebrated by others is essential to the development of a feeling of self-worth and promotes a greater commitment to learning.

- *Learning how to learn*: it is essential that schools encourage young people to develop the capacity to see learning and creative thinking as integral to their experiences and relationships throughout life. Increasingly they are living lives that require them to change and adapt and to recognise that learning is not just a matter of acquiring new information but of making new connections.

There are very many ways in which these experiences can be made real, whatever the context. Sharing responsibility, for example, is more likely to occur in a classroom where working with others is an integral part of the learning and teaching process, since this involves young people in working co-operatively and in making decisions about their own learning. A learning and teaching approach which encourages self and peer assessment encourages young people to begin to reflect on what they are doing and how well they are doing it. It fosters the ability to make informed judgements in other spheres of life. Young people are more likely to be motivated to learn in schools and classrooms that have developed a wide range of strategies for the celebration of achievement. Activities which encourage creative thinking, whatever the knowledge and ideas involved, help develop a more flexible approach to the many situations encountered throughout life.

Essential experiences are also closely bound up with the ethos of the school and the ways in which each pupil feels valued as a learner. They are acted our through the learning and teaching approaches adopted; through the kinds of language and communication used; through the nature of the relationships developed; through the ways in which people behave towards each other; through the attitudes to the environment of the school; and through the relationships developed with parents and the wider community. All teachers should regard it as part of their responsibility to ensure there are opportunities in the learning and teaching process to allow these experiences to happen.

Essential experiences do not easily lend themselves to evaluation by outcomes, yet it is reasonable to ask how schools will know if they are being effective. Evaluating the school as a community of learners is best done in terms of the discernment of tendencies. Students will *tend* to be better able to say for themselves how well they are doing, to work cooperatively, to take autonomous decisions, to find things out for themselves, to display commitment to learning and to the community of the school if these essential experiences form a regular aspect of their learning. The school will *tend* to be a better place to *be*, as well as a better place to work and learn.

Core skills

Learning experiences should also promote the development of what are now variously called key skills or *core skills*. The idea of 'core skills' has been around, especially in the post compulsory and training sectors, for some time. However, it is an imprecise concept open to many, often conflicting, interpretations.

> For example, the term might refer to personal dispositions, mental strategies, accomplished practical routines or a combination of all three. The term does not though, suggest a preference for theoretical, content-specific knowledge.
>
> (Halliday 2000)

Nevertheless, like subjects, core skills as a concept appear to be a fixture and there is a growing international awareness of the relationship between notions of core skills (however described) as a form of essential outcome for education and their location in the curriculum from the earliest stages. Core skills, however, need to be carefully planned and sustained throughout the educational process from pre-school into life-long learning. Such a view implies a new perspective on curriculum planning and also implies that particular attention is given to the significance of frameworks that sustain the integration, continuity and progression of core skills.

In Scotland core skills are defined as Communication, Numeracy, Problem Solving, Information Technology and Working with Others. There can be a temptation to see these as narrowly based and instrumental. For example, 'Working with Others' involves relating well to others, working co-operatively to carry out communal tasks, planning, allocating responsibility, supporting the work of others and reviewing the effectiveness of one's own contribution. These are essentially functional but important aspects of core skill acquisition, allowing us to fulfil a common purpose. Yet, working with others is not just about our functional lives. It is also about our personal lives. We 'work' with others in many dimensions of our lives, as well as in the workplace: in our families, in our social lives, in our relationships. The ability to do this well is a skill of a kind that involves emotional competences – empathy, optimism, resilience – and the interpersonal skills which underpin effective relationships.

> Working with others is, in other words, not just about doing things together, it is also about being together in all kinds of circumstances. Working well together in the sense of sharing a common life is at the heart of any community, and community is essentially an idea built around the quality of relations between people
>
> (Scottish Consultative Council on the Curriculum 1996: v)

Living in harmony depends on being able to work well together. If core skills are to become as important as they should then they must be seen not as 'bolt on' competences, but as a basic dimension of all curriculum planning.

Dispositions

> Schools have an obligation to provide an education for pupils that allows them to acquire the knowledge, skills and qualifications required for a personally rewarding life, productive employment and effective citizenship. Equally schools must set that in a context that encourages learners to develop into fair-minded, considerate and caring human beings. Education must aim to provide a framework on which young people can base critical thinking and judgements. These will enable them to participate as active and responsible citizens in the personal and social dimensions of society, and will encourage them to be explicit about the values of a just and caring society.
>
> (Scottish Consultative Council on the Curriculum, 1995: 1)

The nature and purpose of education cannot simply be described in terms of developing individuals who are efficient, effective and productive: it must develop individuals who are also happy, contented, at peace with themselves and their fellow human beings and hopeful of the future. If the curriculum is to be responsive to the needs of young people and the society in which they live, it must offer opportunities to develop habits of mind and ways of thinking and feeling about the world which will influence positively the ways they are likely to behave towards it, towards themselves and towards other people.

To live purposefully and happily in society and to contribute effectively to it, young people need to become capable of connecting, integrating and applying their personal resources of knowledge, skills and dispositions in creative, thoughtful, sensitive and emotionally mature ways. They need to be able to:

• deal responsibly with their emotions;
• take increasing responsibility for their own lives;
• look after their personal needs, health and safety;
• be sensitive and responsive to the needs of others;
• take responsibility for their learning;
• make decisions based on informed judgements;
• be creative, innovative and enterprising.

Doing well

Perhaps instead of only asking 'What is it that we want our young people to know and be able to do?' we might also ask, 'What does it mean to be human in the twenty first century?' Our job as teachers is to help young people not just to do well in school but to do well in life.

What is done in schools will help to answer that question; answering the question will affect what is done in schools. The essential core understandings that are at the heart of the curriculum are not actually about History, Physical Education or Chemistry, but about transcendent values and transferable skills that will enable young people to make their way in the world with dignity, respect and happiness. If that is accepted the curriculum must be planned and designed around dispositions, capabilities and essential experiences of the kind set out in this chapter. Only then can consideration be given to the organisational features that will best get to these.

> In helping young people and ourselves to learn joyfully as well as effectively, we must remember that the enabling devices of systems and procedures are just that – they are the means which are to be judged by the quality of the human flourishing they promote.
>
> (Fielding 1994: 25)

In a world obsessed with targets, it would be worth setting a target to ensure that young people have opportunities to:

• develop the values and dispositions that are generally acknowledged as fundamental to moral life, a sound guide on which to base personal choice and central to the prospering of a just and democratic society;

- acquire the skills and capabilities essential for life-long learning;
- explore different ways of knowing and different areas of knowledge; and
- develop ways of thinking and feeling about the world which will influence positively how they behave towards it and towards other people.

Implications for teaching

Looking at learning in this way means looking at teaching in a different light. The notion that it is the teacher who is in charge of Oakeshott's 'something in particular' is rarely challenged. But a willingness on the part of teachers to enter into the sort of extended conversations with young people that helps students build their own bridges from present understandings to new and more complex understandings can have a profound effect. Posing questions to challenge students' present conceptions is an important teacher duty. But at the end of the day the significant questions are the ones the students ask themselves.

> Students who frame questions and issues and then go about answering and analysing them take responsibility for their own learning and become problem-solvers and perhaps more importantly problem finders. These students – in pursuit of new understandings – are led by their own ideas and informed by the ideas of others. These students ask for, if not demand, the freedom to play with ideas, explore issues, and encounter new information.
>
> (Brooks and Brooks 1993: 103)

Education for the future

Acquiring dispositions, skills and capabilities, knowledge in the widest sense of the word, and understanding, is at the heart of what it means to be educated. The slogan of educating young people for the future is based on a misconception of the future as a far country we will all eventually arrive in, rather than the sum of all our lives to come. The future is not a monolith that awaits us all, but individual lives as they unfold before us. We cannot predict the future, and therefore, we cannot define it. While educated guesses are possible as to the trends which are likely to affect the contexts in which we will all have to lead our lives, the basic human questions will remain. What is the nature and purpose of human existence? How do we make and sustain relationships with others? What can we make of our lives? How do we deal with our emotions? These are questions that have remained unchanged since the beginning of time. They are also legitimate questions with which education must engage, questions that help all young people to confront their own existences, morality and capacities.

Rarely do we live with one eye on a mythical future. Our lives are lived in all their complexity and ambiguity from day to day. The human scene – the ironies, ambiguities, inconsistencies and contradictions which continually inform our everyday lives – responds to accidents and ideas, to the unforeseen, the unpredictable, to luck both good and bad. All of our futures are unique and multiple. Every day, young people take notice of what is happening around them and over time their minds take in what they notice and in various ways turn what has been witnessed and overheard into their own vision of the world, their own voice.

Young people themselves have much to say on the subject, yet we often neglect to ask them. Students at an Oxford conference on the Curriculum 2000 in April, 1995, were eloquent on their hopes and desires for education. They sought more care and attention from teachers in the conviction that feeling safe leads to better learning. This reflects the conclusions of an earlier report. 'Many students (about 40%) said they had not discussed their work individually with their teachers during this school year' (Keys and Fernandes 1993). The students recognised enjoyment for both students and teachers as an essential element in effective learning. They regarded the relationships that can be developed between students and teachers as all-important. In simpler words this echoes the views of Noddings (1994) who suggests that we should understand education as a series of conversations. The most important of these are special kinds of ordinary conversation that ask three things of teachers. The first is that they are people who try to be good, that is, who consider the effect of their acts on others and respond to difficulties with concern and compassion (even if they don't always bring it off). The second is that they care for children and enjoy their company; and third, they understand that ultimately, the partners in the conversation are more important than the topic, the conclusion or the argument. For these students the most important things that education could do for them was to help them learn how to choose, how to define and pursue their own intellectual agenda, how to take responsibility for their own learning. They regarded the basic essentials in learning as learning how to learn, developing a love of learning, developing self-confidence, trust in their own abilities, and learning how to hold on to their aims.

All too often the aims of education are those of the teachers, not of the learners. We teach young people how to repeat, how to do and, to an unsatisfactory extent, how to learn. What we fail to do is to teach them how to *be* and how to *become* more than they ever thought possible. 'What I don't see here is dreams', said one young student. Education should allow students to leave school with memories which sustain their dignity and sense of inner peace, dreams with which to go forward in life in ways which determine the kind of futures we will all be living in the twenty-first century and the - dispositions and skills to make them real. It must sustain the capacity to wonder and invent, to engage with change and to live happily with it.

The way ahead

In Scotland, The Scottish Executive has set out five purposes of school education. These are to develop young people who are:

- self confident, motivated and well rounded;
- literate and numerate;
- active citizens of a modern democracy;
- enterprising, able to grasp opportunities;
- able to work flexibly.

In England, Ministers have set out three major themes of their vision for education:

- high standards of literacy and numeracy;
- strong moral, personal and social education which prepares children for life as members of a democratic society; and
- a rich and lively experience for children which promotes their eagerness to learn.

(Morris 1997)

The vocabulary is encouraging. The political will may be there. But does the school curriculum as presently constituted shape up to these aims?

We live in a changing world. Wherever we look, the landscape is shifting . . . The world of schools, like everything else, faces the challenges created by such change. It cannot and will not be exempt from the uncertainty that is pervading almost every aspect of life. Preparing young people for the future, for this world of great uncertainty, is amongst the most important and difficult responsibilities faced by society.

(James 1998: 2)

Perhaps the way forward lies in partnership.

Schools do not improve in a climate of threat and sanctions. The metaphor of levering up standards from the outside is a deeply misguided one. Schools improve, just as pupils do, when they are secure and confident enough to be self-critical and when they have the tools and the expertise to evaluate themselves . . . The doors to achievement are locked from the inside. We have to give people the keys to open them from the inside.

(MacBeath 1997)

If the future is *that which will be*, then the future starts now for both schools and students. The purpose of education with integrity is to equip young people with the dispositions, skills, capability, knowledge and ideas to determine for themselves the shape of things to come. In doing so we return education to its rightful place as a moral rather than a technical endeavour and restore to teachers the ethical nuances of their task as educators.

Note

The authors write here in a personal capacity.

References

Bloomer, K. (1999) 'Education in the next Millennium', contribution to The Scotsman Conference, Edinburgh, 1999.

Blythe, T. and Associates (1998) *The Teaching for Understanding Guide*, San Francisco: Jossey-Bass.

Brooks, J.G. and Brooks, M.G. (1993) *In Search of Understanding: the Case for Constructivist Classrooms*, Alexandria VA: Association for Supervision and Curriculum Development.

Coles, R. (1996) *The Mind's Fate: a Psychiatrist Looks at his Profession*, Boston MA: Little, Brown & Co.

Egan, K. (1997) *The Educated Mind: how Cognitive Tools Shape our Understanding*, Chicago: University of Chicago Press.

Eisner, E. W. (1994) *Ethos and Education*, Dundee: Scottish Consultative Committee on the Curriculum.

Entwistle, A. and Entwistle, N. J. (1992) 'Experiences of understanding in revising for degree examinations', *Learning and Instruction*, 2(1): 1–22.

Fielding, M. (1994) 'Delivery, packages and the denial of learning' in H. Bradley, C. Conner and G. Southworth (eds) *Developing Teachers, Developing Schools*, London: David Fulton.

Gardner, H. (1983) *Frames of Mind: the Theory of Multiple Intelligences*, New York: Basic Books.

Gardner, H. (1996) contribution to Second National Conference on Assessing Thinking, Baltimore MD: ASCD.

Gardner, H. (1999) *Conversations with Howard Gardner, An Education for all Human Beings*, http://www.edge.org, Edge.

Halliday, J. (2000) 'Critical thinking and the academic-vocational divide', *The Curriculum Journal*, 11(2): 159–75..

James, L. (1998) *Redefining Schooling: a Challenge to a Closed Society*, London: Royal Society of Arts.

Keys, W. and Fernandes, C. (1993) *What Do Students Think about School?*, Slough: NFER.

MacBeath, J. (1997) 'Hands up all those who think schools get better when threatened by a big stick?', Edinburgh: *Scotland on Sunday*, 29 June 1997.

Morris, E. (1997) Minister of Education Speech at the Primary School Curriculum Conference, London: School Curriculum and Assessment Authority, 10 June 1997.

Noddings, N. (1994) 'Conversation as moral education', *Journal of Moral Education*, 23(2): 107–18.

Oakeshott, M. (1989) *The Voice of Liberal Learning : Michael Oakeshott on Education* (ed. T. Fuller), New Haven: Yale University Press.

Perkins, D. and Blythe, T. (1994) 'Putting understanding up front', *Educational Leadership*, 51(5): 4–7.

Pramling, I. (1990) *Learning to Learn: a Study of Swedish Pre-school Children*, New York: Springer-Verlag.

Rogers, C. and Bateson, G. (1975) *Dialogue on Thinking, Feeling and Learning*, Esalen CA: audiotape published by Association for Supervision and Curriculum Development, Alexandria VA.

Scottish Consultative Council on the Curriculum (1995) *The Heart of the Matter*, Dundee: Scottish Consultative Council on the Curriculum.

Scottish Consultative Council on the Curriculum (1996) *Working with Others*, Dundee: Scottish Consultative Council on the Curriculum.

Whitehead, A. N. (1948) *Science and the Modern World*, New York: New America Library.

5 'Now just compose yourselves' – personal development and integrity in changing times

Chris Watkins

In this chapter I consider personal development in modern times. The focus is mainly on young people and their development, but I start by discussing how such development is conceived. The idea I want to exercise is that we think about personal development in an outdated way, more suited to the Victorian era or the factory age. Nowadays our conception needs to change, to include better understandings of the lives young people lead, the way they learn and how they may compose a life. Central to all of that is a different view of what personal integrity should come to mean, in both the senses explored in this book: how will 'wholeness' develop, and how will 'uprightness' emerge? There will be plenty of implications for the role of schools and I hope to spell out key ones.

Introduction: reviewing our metaphors for development

First I wish to examine the taken-for-granted ways in which we currently conceive personal development. When we talk in day-to-day terms about this theme we do not use a particular specialised language: instead we talk in a way which uses images from a range of other sources. Our conception of what 'growing up' means, what supports it, and what are its end points, is constructed through various metaphors – pictures from somewhere else which we use to describe and illuminate the theme. This is not an unusual phenomenon when we discuss complex social matters. For example, the various metaphors we live by have been analysed (Lakoff and Johnson 1980), and our formal understandings of organisations are well arranged under various metaphors (Morgan 1986).

I offer a personal collection of five significant metaphors for personal development, and hope to illuminate the particular picture on which each depends. In trying to 'bring these pictures to life' I include some of the everyday sayings and wisecracks which may relate to them.

- Development as settling down, even 'buckling down' – becoming fastened to something serious. This conjures up the idea that the process is one of subordinating youthful interests and 'drives' in order to arrive at an end-state characterised by a patterned repertoire, which might include the acceptance of current social norms. Settling down also calls to mind the process of sedimentation. This metaphor implies a corresponding view of adulthood: as economic agent (regular breadwinner), as moral agent (s/he who has come to know best) and psychological agent (who has forged an identity through the blooming confusion of adolescence in which internal drives and external constraints are in combat). Adults sometimes express envy created by this image, and remark 'youth is wasted on the young'.

- Development as growth, maturation, expansion. Here the person is viewed in their biological aspect, which of course may be accurate for describing the organic growth and later decline, but the metaphor is extended to the psychological and social. The picture created is of progressive development which seems 'natural': the corollary is that it may become stunted if insufficiently fed. 'Home is the place where teenagers go to refuel.'

- Development as a process of passing through identifiable stages. This characterisation has been used by some psychologists who describe developmental stages, each with characteristic ways of being and comprising a necessary preparation for the next. It has also been used by some sociologists who describe different age-related periods in terms of different legal, cultural and role expectations. 'He's going through his adolescent phrase.'

- Development as a journey. This metaphor brings with it ideas of plans and goals: planning the journey, identifying where we want to reach. Here we talk about 'equipping' or 'preparing' young people for adult life, 'getting a good start', 'helping them find a direction' and so on. The image of the road to the future is a strong one. As one parent commented: 'She's stopped asking where she's come from and started to refuse to tell us where she's going.'

- Development as choosing a vocation. A broad notion of vocation can signify becoming a something – a job, a role, an adult. Adulthood is portrayed as the important state, so that the young person is an adult-in-waiting. But the other element of this metaphor, the idea of choice, can go unnoticed. The classic question: 'What do you want to be when you grow up?' reflects this conception, and the idea that preference for future role will answer everything about personal development. A wisecrack from this view is 'Teenagers today know everything – except how to make a living.'

Together, these images start to unearth the underlying view that development is a process of achieving consistency, significance, sameness and some sort of end-state. But as you read, some flaws might have started to appear in their descriptive power, and a lack of fit with the times in which we currently live. For example:

- Development as settling down. The notion that adult patterns of life are settled has been questioned for an increasing proportion of the population: in post-industrial society adults experience many changes. The associated view of young people simply adopting static values from their environment is increasingly shown to be erroneous: they are involved in adaptation and change, and are sometimes part of much wider patterns in value change. Their experience of development is not one of conflict, or 'storm and strife' as a prelude to consistency – though this might describe the family dynamics for the minority who engage with therapeutic help (Haley 1980).

- Development as growth and maturation. The apparent smoothness of growth in this image contrasts with the non-linear, erratic sense of development which characterises it for many. Defining moments in a life are often the unexpected crises and the unprepared-for transitions. Sometimes adolescents go through transformational changes which this metaphor might underestimate: for example, loss of a parent, moving from the parental home, an accident, a lottery win or even appearance on a TV confessional show. When disequilibrium happens, and a change of state occurs, an element of the random enters in. Adopting a vegetation metaphor, with its agenda for optimal growth, misses the point.

- Development as passing through stages. This metaphor has been challenged by evidence from both ends of the life span: first, young people are often capable of the functioning which was supposed to characterise later stages and, second, many adults do not consistently behave according to the characteristics attributed to that stage. Stage theories may have under-estimated young people's capacities, and over-estimated differences between young people and adults (David, this volume). Trajectories are not so predictable: 'a virtual infinity of developmental forms seems possible, and which particular form emerges may depend on a confluence of particulars, the existence of which is fundamentally unsystematic' (Gergen, 1982: 161).

- Development as going on a journey. The 'maps' for creating a life in modern times are not for sale at the road-side: pathways to jobs and to success are not clear, setting a clear direction may be a recipe for disappointment, and which equipment is needed for the journey is now contested. Whereas up to the mid-twentieth century much of the knowledge required to manage adult life was gained through school, now a much smaller proportion is available through that experience.

- Development as choosing a vocation or job. The notion of a 'job for life' has disappeared in most sectors of employment, and with it has gone a predictable view of the qualifications or previous experience needed to gain access. Indeed the extent to which job advertisements specify qualifications has reduced in recent years, in favour of personal characteristics, working style and attitude to learning. The idea that people choose freely and supposedly 'rationally' from a range of options is known to be wide of the mark. And with the increase in life expectancy, jobs become a smaller proportion of everyone's life.

Each metaphor may have existed for centuries, but the historical social and cultural conditions of particular times may have focused them. While not wishing to promote simplistic versions of history, I speculate the following particular worlds of ideas for the above five. Development as settling down may be drawn from the invention of thermodynamics (the predecessor of psychodynamics) and the growth of industry, giving us images of force and pressure needing external control to create the stable state. Development as growth and maturation may derive from thinking about evolution and from 'normal' biology, the growth of food crops and the 'normal distribution' in statistics, which originated in that field. Development as passing through identifiable stages mirrors the times of defining civic duties, the introduction of age-graded schooling and the invention of adolescence. Development as going on a journey calls up romantic notions of travel and exploration, occasionally extending to images of crusades, colonialism, or the Grand Tour, while development as choosing a vocation or job derives from the industrial revolution, expansion of work and the partial democratisation of jobs achieved by merit rather than ascription.

The historical location of our current metaphors may show their lack of fit to current times, and also reveal other reservations. As with many other images which we retain from our past, they may apply most to the dominant but minority groups of their time. Patterns of gender and class are not far beneath the surface. They may have applied less to the majority of lives, and even for the dominant minority they were probably over-simplifications.

Our current metaphors have impact: they are more than passing descriptions. They influence the way that we describe, understand and respond to issues where they are invoked. Although their permeation of everyday talk leads us not to notice our unwitting attachment, they play a part in our construction of our realities.

Changing times, changing metaphors?

As the world changes, our ways of understanding and our metaphors may also change. However in times of change, old metaphors could maintain a conservative impact by impeding the recognition and acceptance of change. For example, when someone takes a view that development is not happening according to their expectations, the above metaphors are used actively. Minor moral panics are constructed and particular fears are voiced in terms which contain these images:

- young people not settling down, being 'wild';
- youth being immature;
- adolescents as irresponsible;
- young people getting stuck, or being direction-less; and
- 'he's got no idea of what he wants to be'.

For some individual young people, such statements can indicate real difficulties, but when used more broadly these phrases regularly cast young people as deviant in society, on occasions when they would not themselves be experiencing a felt difficulty. How can we make sense of this phenomenon? At one level it is one generation showing its use of out-dated metaphors for understanding the development of the next generation. This can be seen at the smallest scale in family processes: parents of adolescents are likely to use scripts in relating to their adolescents which their parents used in relating to them, and we know that the period when young people and their families address the independence issue is the time when families most seek help (Haley 1980). In the larger domain of power and social control, these images sustain past ways of thinking and make existing constructions of reality difficult to break, so that current power relations are maintained through their use. Examples are to be found in the discourse of politicians and other moral entrepreneurs (Cohen 1973) who become engaged in heated ways about 'the youth question', predicting dire consequences for society if young people's deviance is not addressed and 'corrected'.

The process of pathologising youth and its development is not new, and the metaphors in use may always have changed over time, so is there any particular value in highlighting this process now? I think so. Currently the pace of change seems significantly increased, and metaphors (which are always slow to change) may now become conservative forces more quickly than before. I see this in the increasingly broad way that deviance is still attributed to the young at the beginning of the twenty-first century. There seem fewer occasions of appreciation and regard, in a general atmosphere more characterised by compliance and control. So rather than a general recognition and acceptance of change, the usual targets are pathologised.

On some occasions the recognition that things are changing is voiced, yet this in turn creates worries rather than acceptance. It may be that fears of the future are easy to stimulate if and when people feel that they cannot take sufficient of the known into the unknown. For example, the old ways of describing personal development, which emphasised sameness and consistency, might be recognised as outdated, but an acceptable alternative is not yet available. So we hear people voicing a deeper set of fears about young people's development – that it will degenerate into individualism and relativism. I think we need not jump to that other extreme.

We need ideas which might stand us in better stead for thinking about the development of young people in the current context, and these ideas will need to incorporate more of what we know about that context. Since such ideas will be relatively new, they may not link to an available metaphor in our language, but they may resonate with the wisecrack 'The problems of the world today are so complex that even teenagers don't have the answer.'

The metaphors for development also imply our beliefs about how integrity is achieved. If we are in a context where old predictabilities now seem less valid, what will it mean to have a sense of coherence to person-hood and to life? The challenge is to leave behind old certainties which have become unsafe, and seek safe uncertainties in what is emerging. In these times when change is apparent on social, technological, economic, ecological and political dimensions, it would seem a logical corollary that the dynamics of personal identity will also change.

In the remainder of this chapter I will consider growing up as composing a life in complex and increasingly fast-moving ways, in which the processes of learning and advancing complexity will be central themes. I also indicate how a new understanding of personal integrity emerges.

Personal development and the development of complexity

Metaphors from the industrial age and the romantic era, which privileged sameness and consistency in the person, are now less tenable, so how can we conceptualise development, and what constitutes progression? Here I remember the words of a noted headteacher and public figure, at an otherwise boring seminar on personal–social education, saying 'the issues and dilemmas I face now at 60 are fundamentally the same as the ones that I experienced at 15 – but the complexity is probably different'. As a key guiding concept, complexity has been identified as a characteristic of advances in many fields of intellectual endeavour (Waldrop 1994), and in some ways has been applied in understanding persons.

Csikszentmihalyi (1990) has studied optimal experiences in everyday life, in a wide range of people from champion figure skaters and Navajo shepherds to Japanese teenage motorcycle racers and chess masters. Common features have been identified. Optimal experiences are characterised by 'flow', episodes of concentration, absorption, deep involvement, joy, and a sense of accomplishment. These occur in situations of high challenge and high skill. Some people, including some young people, achieve higher proportions of flow in everyday life than do others. Such people are likely to set goals, have surplus psychic energy to invest in everyday experience, and do things for their own sake rather than in order to achieve some later goal. Adolescents who are characterised in this way 'learn to experience flow by getting involved in activities that are more likely to provide it, namely mental work and active leisure' (Csikszentmihalyi 1997: 120).

With this background, Csikszentmihalyi also considers the processes of personal development as the development of complexity. Complexity is an increase in both differentiation and integration. Differentiation refers to the degree to which elements of a system differ from each other. Integration refers to the extent to which elements of a system are connected with each other. A system that is more differentiated and integrated than another is said to be more complex. Increased complexity is the goal of much important learning, in which fine-grain differentiation can be made at the same time as understanding much wider integration of concepts. It is in a similar vein to the notion that in the process of learning what is learned is variation (Marton and Booth 1997). It reminds us that earlier theories which emphasised differentiation in identity formation were only highlighting part of the picture: difference and connection must both develop.

Domains of complexity in personal development

From the perspective of developing complexity, personal development can be considered in a number of domains. I propose to discuss three: interpersonal repertoire, sense of self or selves and interpersonal relations.

Descriptions of another person have tended to reflect the perspective of an outside observer. We describe the other in terms such as they're this or that sort of person, whereas we explain our own behaviour by referring to the context or circumstances. An effect of this has been the tendency to talk of others in ways which emphasise them as self-standing individuals, separate from context and from relations. This is also reflected in the grand narratives of philosophers' 'what does it mean to be a person?' and the static 'characteristics' or 'virtues' which that discourse gave us.

In order to reflect better the interpersonal rather than the personal, a more dynamic way of describing is needed, something which emphasises the person in relation. We might conceptualise the person as their cluster of relationships, thinking of them as a node in a web of relationships. Similarities and differences in the features of this web (its extent, the quality of relationship, degree of connectedness and so on) turn out to make sense of many important similarities and differences between people, of the changes that may occur in their lives, and also of how change can be made in their lives. In an analysis of contemporary life and the changes since the romantic age and the modern age, Gergen (1991) has suggested that the very idea of individual selves each possessing mental qualities is now threatened with eradication. Our relational embeddedness is crucial, which leads to a focus on interpersonal repertoire.

A young person's interpersonal repertoire could be considered in terms of its range and complexity, and development viewed as increasing the complexity of situations encountered and handled. This would reflect what we know about our changing context: according to Gergen 'the number and variety of relationships in which we are engaged, potential frequency of contact, expressed intensity of relationship, and endurance through time are all steadily increasing' (1991: 61) mainly as a result of the technologies of the century such as travel, film and the explosion in communication technologies. In this increasingly saturated situation, the variety of contexts in which we find ourselves has an impact on identity: the wider range of different contexts triggers people to be suddenly propelled by a wider range of alternative impulses. 'They seem securely to be one sort of person, but yet another comes bursting to the surface – in a private activity or a turn of interests' (*ibid.*: 68). One of his examples: You work as an executive in the investments department of a bank. In the evenings you smoke marijuana and listen to Grateful Dead.

The experience of increased variation promotes the acquisition of multiple and disparate potentials for being. Our conceptions become not an individual self, but multiple selves, each with relations and contexts; not solid centres and unified wholes, but constructions in their different contexts. Young people often convey the sense of inhabiting multiple worlds, in ways which may reflect what adults are now coming to re-discover in fast-changing times. Markus and Nurius (1986) have described how important dynamics of the person may be viewed in terms of the dynamics between aspects of multiple selves.

In this context is there a new notion of integrity? If the notion of a simple sameness is given up, will multiplicity only engender self-contradiction? I think not, because the shift is away from self as object, and towards thinking of self as process, and reconstructing self as relationship. As a result our sense of multiple selves can build a coherence which is not a static one. Connectedness for the person is likely to derive from the dynamic qualities of the relationships and narratives which are constructed, and the goals and futures they embody. This is an alternative view to the potentially reductionist 'developing social skills': although enhanced skills may play their part in areas such as handling change and accepting safe uncertainties, this is likely to feel an outmoded contribution, since adding a skill seems somehow less than expanding a life.

A focus on relationships may be extended from young people's selves through community connectedness, to wider societal collaboration. Here the notion of trust takes on a special significance, as a concept for describing pro-social aspects of relationships and illuminating how society functions. Fukuyama (1995) has analysed how wider layers of trust, from family through civic society to state, are related to key concerns such as the economic performance of countries. Sadly in Britain the expressed level of general trust in society has fallen since the 1960s (Abramson and Inglehart 1995). Nevertheless, the move from individual selves to multiple selves and relations, with the person exercising increased linkage through communications, requires a new conception of progression. Rather than the stage-defined individualist beliefs of the modern age, progression in interpersonal relations might come to be seen as the increasing complexity of contributions a person's relations make to the development of trust. A person might ask of themselves or of others 'what have my relations added to the commonwealth?'.

The contribution of interpersonal relationships to community and trust may also address the fears of fragmentation which are currently strong in many people's views of the future (Watkins 1996). Social exclusion and division are concomitants of strong individualism: the relational perspective offers more inclusion and a distributed definition of progress. It may also lead to a relational view of morality, and of moral uprightness, that second sense of integrity. If morality is removed from the heads of individuals, it can be conceptualised as a relational phenomenon of contribution to a common good, contributing to a relational or communal benefit.

So the relational self contributes to a dynamic new complexity of social cohesion and to a new more networked than hierarchical form of social capital. This is where a further analysis offered by Csikszentmihalyi (1993) links complexity with harmony. In evolutionary terms, simple individual selves try to control far more energy than his/her biological system requires for survival, whereas complex relational selves may require less energy than biological drives would prompt him/her to acquire. This idea bears similarity to the distinction between belongingness identities and process identities (Curle 1972). The distinction suggested that those young people who defined themselves in terms of what belonged to them or what they belonged to, engaged in different forms of social action from those who defined themselves in terms of their here-and-now processes and priorities. It also raises the theme of materialism in personal development and identity. Kress (1995) suggests that 'The world of tomorrow may offer its inhabitants a lesser level of material well-being, and yet an at least equal and perhaps greater level of satisfaction.' This certainly provides a more attractive vision than the scenario of future disintegration. But how could it be? Evidence in Western Europe suggests that there is a consistent shift, generation by generation, towards what Ingelhart (1990, 1997) has termed 'post-material values'. This is a 'shift from emphasis on economic and physical security above all, toward greater emphasis on belonging, self-expression, and the quality of life' (1990: 11). And contrary to views which are heard from some commentators and some teachers, 'the basic values of contemporary youth are not more materialistic than those of their counterparts a decade or two earlier'. Indeed the value map of British society (Synergy Brand Values 1994) suggests that young people are developing the values needed for these changing times and to suit them for the future world, i.e. the leading edge values include androgyny, internationalism, balance, complexity and excitement. These values are a reflection of their identity formation rather than a simple outgrowth of what has been 'passed on' to them.

Will tomorrow's schools embrace such a perspective and will they leave behind the too simple notion of consistency which currently underlies their practices? Can they support young people in the development of multiple selves and help them forge complexity? On occasion encouragement to seek diversity, to extend range, and to be non-standard will be needed! Schools will need to regain their ability to expand the number of perspectives on a given question and help young people actively choose the option that will enhance complexity. They will need to help young people prepare for what is not known. Can our schools enhance the development of such values, and celebrate complexity and connectedness? Can they recognise that the new values which are emerging do not put young people into conflict with the preceding generations? Instead they offer increased synergy at the exact time when societal development needs it. Young people seek new forms of belonging, experience or attachment in a fast-expanding scene.

It is no coincidence that this discussion has started to focus on the future. If multiple selves, multiple relations and multiple contexts are the order of the day, then their dynamics are importantly informed and influenced by what Markus and Nurius (1986) have described as 'possible selves'. These are the multiple conceptions people hold of what they might become, would like to become, or are afraid to become. This surely is something which school experience should be able to enhance – the constructive development of possible selves and the goals to match.

Goals and their social nature are crucial to a dynamic integrity. Studies of social competence have highlighted key elements: goal-directedness, an interest in social goals, and ideas about improvement. Using a very open and contextual view of social competence, Ford concludes: 'Adolescents who are judged as able to behave effectively in challenging situations . . . assign relatively high priorities to interpersonal goals (such as helping others, getting socially involved, and getting along with parents and friends) and are likely to describe themselves as possessing the intrapersonal resources to accomplish these goals. They also tend to be more goal-directed than their peers' (1982: 340). This conclusion links with the conclusion from Csikszentmihalyi: the person who can set goals, become involved, and direct their attention gains most from immediate experience, and in the context of others is open to enhancing those gains with others.

Can schools help young people to become proactive and diverse in their personal goal-setting? This would be a far more impactful contribution than the current scene of defining the goals of schooling as exam performance and promoting limited forms of target-setting. It would need to recognise that personal effectiveness now includes a sense of goal-setting which includes doing things for their own sake rather than for some deferred achievement. This may be asking schools to give up too much: the beliefs in 'delaying gratification' are no less strong just because they are out-dated. It requires the radical shift to learning as a way of being, rather than learning as a means to doing (Vaill 1996). Puritan fears of young people as hedonistic would doubtless emerge and have to be handled, but they are clearly a product of a previous age.

So where's the future for young people in schools?

With this provocative question, I am not asking about young people's prospects after they leave school, nor about the prospects for the future of schools (although both are good questions). Here I am considering how and when the experience of school stimulates and supports young people in thinking ahead to their own futures.

People who function effectively and with satisfaction in the modern world have a developed attitude towards the future. This is not to say they have a fixed attitude, but they do consider and embrace the future and what it may bring, thereby constructing hope. The contrast is the various pathologies of the future: denying it, ignoring it, narrowing it, over-planning it. Boscolo and Bertrando (1993) have clarified that many aspects of well-functioning families can be traced to the developed and synchronous views of family members regarding time and the future. Karniol and Ross (1996) have reviewed the psychology of time orientations and Binks (2000) has developed evidence that teachers who are proactive and comfortable about their futures are more effective classroom managers and learners in their own right. A vision of the future is also influential on wider social relations and connections. Axelrod (1990) demonstrated that the conditions for people cooperating with each other (without a third party telling them to) included that each party could see the future implications of their actions on the other, and in this way the 'shadow of the future' fell back on to the current behaviour. As the pace of change increases we grow more frustrated with stories of the past, and in this context people who are comfortable with their future are well suited to their context. Yet the current condition of our schools seems to offer little or no stimulus for young people to develop a view on the future, in its personal and broader senses. The curriculum is overcrowded with subject knowledge generated by previous generations. The styles of pedagogy which are officially encouraged are about instruction rather than construction or co-construction. The end purposes have been narrowed to a view of performance indicated through public examination results. This will need to change for schools to have a future.

What would we need to see in any school which helped young people develop their future orientation? Some of the elements would be extensions of the themes encountered in this discussion: the extension of multiple selves to possible selves, the promotion of appropriate goal-setting rather than target-setting, and helping young people develop how their contribution will make a difference. Extending these into the core theme of composing a life would mean helping young people develop their reflexivity, their knowledge of selves in relation to context, and their future orientation through exploring questions such as:

- What might your life be like in ten years' time?
- When might you be ready to leave home?
- When might your parents accept you are able to go?
- How might you make a difference to the world you live in?
- What will matter most for you in composing a life?
- How will you be in the world you wish to see?

As schools help young people learn about themselves in contexts, and about how social systems beyond the family work, they make a major contribution to personal development. Through the forms of social and learning relations which are created in school, and in the relations with social systems beyond the school, they have the potential for contributing greatly to young people's complexity and resilience for an unknown but certainly changing future. There is much to be done in updating schools to the changed world. Tomorrow's schools need to play a significant part in the future, and in regard to personal development their motto could usefully be to help young people compose a life and make a difference.

References

Abramson, P. R. and Inglehart, R. (1995) *Value Change in Global Perspective*, Ann Arbor: University of Michigan Press.

Axelrod, R. (1990) *The Evolution of Cooperation*, London: Penguin.

Binks, P. (2000) *Teacher Biographies, Teachers' Development and Development Strategies*, PhD in progress, University of London Institute of Education.

Boscolo, L. and Bertrando, P. (1993) *The Times of Time: a New Perspective in Systemic Therapy and Consultation*, New York: W. W. Norton.

Cohen, S. (1973) *Folk Devils and Moral Panics*, St Albans: Paladin.

Csikszentmihalyi, M. (1990) *Flow: the Psychology of Optimal Experience*, New York: Harper & Row.

Csikszentmihalyi, M. (1993) *The Evolving Self: a Psychology for the Third Millennium*, New York: Harper Collins.

Csikszentmihalyi, M. (1997) *Finding Flow: the Psychology of Engagement with Everyday Life*, New York: Basic Books.

Curle, A. (1972) *Mystics and Militants: a Study of Awareness, Identity and Social Action*, London: Tavistock.

Ford, M. E. (1982) 'Social cognition and social competence in adolescence', *Developmental Psychology*, 18: 323–40.

Fukuyama, F. (1995) *Trust: the Social Virtues and the Creation of Prosperity*, New York: Free Press.

Gergen, K. J. (1982) *Toward Transformation in Social Knowledge*, New York: Springer-Verlag.

Gergen, K. J. (1991) *The Saturated Self*, New York: Basic Books.

Haley, J. (1980) *Leaving Home*, New York: McGraw-Hill.

Hoffman, L. (1992) 'A reflexive stance for family therapy' in S. McNamee and K. J. Gergen (eds) *Therapy as Social Construction*, London: Sage.

Inglehart, R. (1990) *Culture Shift in Advanced Industrial Society*, Princeton NJ: Princeton University Press.

Inglehart, R. (1997) *Modernization and Postmodernization: Cultural, Economic, and Political Change in 43 Countries*, Princeton NJ: Princeton University Press.

Karniol, R. and Ross, M. (1996) 'The motivational impact of temporal focus – thinking about the future and the past', *Annual Review of Psychology*, 47: 593–620.

Kress, G. (1995) *Writing the Future: English and the Making of a Culture of Innovation*, Sheffield: National Association for the Teaching of English.

Lakoff, G. and Johnson, M. (1980) *Metaphors We Live By*, Chicago: University of Chicago Press.

Markus, H. and Nurius, P. (1986) 'Possible selves', *American Psychologist*, 41(9): 954–69.

Marton, F. and Booth, S. (1997) *Learning and Awareness*, Mahwah NJ: Lawrence Erlbaum.

Morgan, G. (1986) *Images of Organisation*, Thousand Oaks CA: Sage Publications.

Synergy Brand Values (1994) 'Insight '94' Trend map, cited in H. Wilkinson (1994) *No Turning Back: Generations and the Genderquake*, London: DEMOS.

Vaill, P. B. (1996) *Learning as a way of Being: Strategies for Survival in a World of Permanent White Water*, San Francisco: Jossey-Bass.

Waldrop, M. M. (1994) *Complexity: the Emerging Science at the Edge of Order and Chaos*, London: Penguin.

Watkins, C. (1996) 'Re-imagining Affective Learning in and for a Fragmented Future', paper presented at European Union Affective Education Conference: 'Touching the Future', Marino Institute of Education, Dublin. <www.ioe.ac.uk/agel/Marino_EU_paper.html>

6 Stand and deliver – the teacher's integrity?

John Sullivan

Deliver

1 save, rescue, set free (from).

2 assist at birth of or in giving birth; give birth to . . .; unburden oneself (of opinion etc.) in discourse.

3 give up or over, abandon, resign, hand on to another; distribute . . . hand over formally . . .

4 launch, aim, (blow, ball, attack); (of judge) pronounce (judgement); utter, recite . . .
[ME, f. OF *delivrer* f. Gallo-Rom. *deliberare* (as DE-, L *liberare* LIBERATE)]

The sea of stories

I'm often asked what it's like being a teacher. I've used many different answers to this, ranging from 'often frustrating but never dull' to 'it's better than selling insurance', largely depending on my level of morale. My current favourite reply is: 'I'm in too many stories.' It sounds a little melodramatic, but how else can one convey the nature of a job so crowded with narratives?

As a classroom teacher I have access to around 180 students' personal and academic narratives, revealed as I interact with them, teach them, mark their work. As Head of Department, add about another hundred or so: the stories of students referred to me for a variety of reasons. Then there are the adult narratives of the nine colleagues I manage, plus the multi-fold narratives of the staff-room and various staff forums: the micro- and macropolitics of the school (Ball 1990).

There are the narratives of whole classes' relationships and progress. There are the narratives of year groups, of key stages. There are the narratives of development work in the department. There are the narratives of whole-school initiatives. Then the local picture: the stories within the local education authority of catchments and competition.

The national picture adds further narratives of government initiatives, decrees and inspections. Some of these stories are happy – the majority of them are not. Perhaps it is the cumulative weight of the stories teachers live in that makes them feel burdensome. The good stories become obscured by the bad: when one student's personal problems are resolved, another crisis appears; when one class makes good progress, another has difficulty; when one initiative is up and running, another appears; a set of good examination results merely adds pressure on the next cohort.

For the external narratives add extra weight. In the increasingly data-rich environment of education, the internal narratives of students' and teachers' lives become irrelevant in the face of a cold question asked by external examinations and inspection: *in terms of the national picture, are students making the progress that they should?* When we are asked this question, by a manager or by an inspector, complex local narratives cannot be offered as context or justification. We are expected to have dealt with them and to have *delivered*. For our job is, ultimately, to *deliver* the curriculum and to *deliver* results.

Here, *deliver* can have one meaning only. As a letter or email arrives on the mat or PC, or a pizza arrives at our door, so the knowledge, skills and understanding required by external assessments has, one hopes, arrived on candidates' papers and the figures required by government, governors or headteacher have arrived on the relevant desks. The meta-narrative of result-defined 'effectiveness' dominates the narratives of the daily landscape of teaching.

In class

What happens to teachers near examination time? We cram. We stand and deliver. We teach students to jump through hoops whose dimensions we have not set. In class there are ever-increasing pressures on teachers to *deliver* according to sense 3 only: teaching is seen as the 'handing over formally' of the curriculum (therefore tending to sense 4: we 'aim' and expect students to 'recite' in turn). Resultant pedagogies lead to crude *ventriloquy*: students learn to be operated by academic discourses rather than operating them.

As an illustration, here is the story of a recent Monday.

During Lesson One, I ask five 13 year-olds to write a hierarchical Person Specification for their ideal teacher. Unanimously voted Quality Number One is *someone who listens*. Number Two is *someone who explains clearly*. Number Three is *someone who allows us our own opinions.* It is a heartening start to the week. I make silent vows.

I then spend Lesson Two with a low-ability class finishing coursework for their imminent GCSE examinations in English. I ask them what they think of *Macbeth* and assume the listening position. They ask me to tell them what to think so they can write it down and hand it back to me. The votive candles splutter.

Lesson Three is a meeting with the Headteacher. I have just submitted targets for the department's end of Key Stage Three external assessments. We appear to have committed ourselves to a three per cent increase on last year's results with an arguably weaker cohort. I leave his office and march down the corridor calculating how many lessons we have left with that year group before the examinations.

Lesson Four is with that very year group. I pinch their noses and ladle the content into them. Restlessly they copy yet another exam-technique mantra from the board. One of them asks me: 'When are we going to *do* something?' By and large, they indulge my panic. I have a growing sensation that I am selling them short.

Why was it so difficult for me to adhere to the vows of Lesson One? That is how I want to teach: I know it is the best way. Yet what I want to do, or can do, or think is best becomes subordinate to doing what I'm told. The stories I tell myself about my teaching are edited out under pressure from the stories I'm told about *delivery*.

Here's the rub: in theory we have shared goals with assessment authorities, with examination boards, with school management and colleagues. In an ideal world, we work towards shared goals by diverse means: that alchemic mixture of teacher individualism and common aims (Stoll and Fink 1996: 96–7). Yet there is undoubtedly a sense in which teacher autonomy is being constrained. The goals – whether we agree with them or not – are dictated: no room for autonomy there. There is an increasing tendency to specify not only learning objectives and outcomes, but teaching methods too, exemplified by the National Literacy Strategy at KS2 and KS3. While these policies are marketed as spreading best practice, what inevitably occurs is a perception that, despite talk of consultation and partnership, the empowered movement is one way. The tablets are handed down; Government delivers policy to Local Education Authorities; Local Education Authorities deliver policy via training to schools; teachers deliver in the classroom. Conflict and dis-ease thus arise at all levels: from the relationship between government and LEAs to the interaction between headteachers and staff, subject leaders and colleagues, teachers and students, teachers and parents.

In schools and teams

The 'rightness' of the diktat is irrelevant. What matters is its *exteriority*. Bakhtin (1981) argues that there are two competing forces within cultures. The first is the natural inclination towards diversity and difference: the centrifugal force that throws us to the edges, creating regional, subcultural and individual variations. The second force is centripetal: that centralising, unifying hegemonic force that plays down or eradicates regional or subcultural differences and emphasises homogeneity. In education, as we have seen, centripetal forces or external narratives apply increased and increasing pressure upon teachers and schools.

There seem to be only two possible reactions. Centripetal, unifying forces militate against liminal or radical identity, so teachers must either succumb to the centripetal force and become orthodox or, in order to retain their oppositional, resistant identity, must withdraw further to the edge and re-form themselves in a more heretical, more radical image.

For the latter, surely, the result is *dis*-identification with the hegemony: the creation of heretical subcultures. For some, working in schools may be defined in terms of a modernist struggle between dominance and subordinacy, between oppressor and oppressed, between them and us. 'Them' is, variously, the government, the school inspectorate, the governing body, the headteacher, the management team, the subject leader, the students. These 'heretical' teachers become the 'Armageddon brigade': the disaffected complainers who gather in sequestered sites, hissing dissent.[1] They are defined not by *resistance*, which implies conflict over specifics, but by *reactance*, which implies constant opposition regardless of subject. Such reactance is not just sour grapes, but a struggle against orthodoxy at all costs, as struggle is intrinsic to oppositional identity. How some teachers become reactant will be explored below.

For those who opt for orthodoxy, working in schools can become a form of acceptance, of tired trooperism, of further grudging ventriloquy. Teachers feel operated by external diktats and sets of assumptions about their work and thus themselves that delimit and inhibit; that enforce at least superficial or partial adherence to this year's new initiative, that reinforce 'them and us' dialectics. The principles, the goals, the rationales, are no longer ours, but theirs: the methods increasingly so, too. How can teachers be fulfilled, or even happy, when their actions are dictated by others?

Thus many staff-rooms become subsistence cultures: we discuss how to get by, not how to move on. Work becomes a set of short-term problems to deal with, a serving machine that keeps the balls coming at us, while we run from baseline to net, desperately swatting them back. We talk about paperwork. We talk about problem students. We talk about workload, about not re-inventing the wheel. We rail against the latest external initiative. We rarely talk about *teaching*. Should a more conceptual issue be raised at a meeting, it is as if old wounds were being opened or new injuries too terrifying to contemplate were imminent, and the issue is passed over.

Is this silence our response to external pressures, or to the vague and conflicting goals of teaching, a bid to bury the issues rather than attempt to allow for pluralism? The answer is that we are riddled with self-doubt about our abilities. It is easier to talk practice, not praxis. Re-reading how Lieberman and Miller explore the notion of the 'practical' as opposed to the theoretical or 'idealistic' produces a chilly *frisson* of recognition:

> Practical school problems include discipline, attendance, order, achievement. Practical ideas require little additional work or preparation; they fit in to the existing rhythms of the school. Practical ideas are immediate and concrete and can be effected with the resources and structures that currently exist. . . . 'we do the best we can in the circumstances'. . . . To be practical means to . . . draw on experience rather than research . . . to accept the school as it is . . . Striving to change the system is idealistic; striving to make do is practical. Concern for each student's well-being and optimal learning is idealistic; acceptance of limitations of student potential and teacher influence is practical. Reflective self-criticism is idealistic; expressing the belief 'I do the best I can; it's just that the kids don't try' is practical. Being open to change . . . is idealistic; being self-sufficient is practical. Being practical saves one from shame and doubt. It is a useful rule to follow. . . . By following the privacy rule teachers forfeit the opportunity to display their successes; but they also gain. They gain the security of not having to face their failures publicly and losing face.
>
> (1991: 158)

So, by focusing on procedures and not principles we shore ourselves up. This is a 'defensive routine' we utilise to protect ourselves, because we feel threatened and vulnerable (Morgan, 1987: 89). Any 'idealism' of individual members of the team tends to be conveyed in secret huddles, away from the collegial space. Within many staff-rooms the assumption is that the common denominator is the lowest bearable. The culture we construct is one of making do, not making good: *copeability*, not *capability*. If one accepts Darling-Hammond's definition of teacher professionalism as

> [doing] whatever is best for the client, not what is easiest or most expedient . . . [basing] a decision . . . on available knowledge – not just that knowledge acquired from personal experience but also on . . . research knowledge
>
> (Darling-Hammond 1990: 92)

then copeability leads to de-professionalisation. Indeed, many teachers' conversations tend towards topics identified by Rosenholtz as those favoured by 'low-efficacy teachers' (Rosenholtz 1991: 85). Terrified by the prospect that open debate about goals or methods would unleash the centrifugal forces and spin us into chaos, what are by nature pluralist organisations nurture impersonations of unitary teams.

According to Morgan a unitary organisation 'places emphasis on the achievement of common objectives . . . [and] regards conflict as a rare and transient phenomenon'. A pluralist organisation 'places emphasis on the diversity of individual and group interests . . . regards conflict as an inherent and in-eradicable characteristic of organisational affairs and stresses its potentially positive or functional aspects' (1997: 199–208).

Are schools and departments within schools unitary or pluralist? Ball's (1990) exploration of school culture is based upon the premise that 'schools, in common with virtually all other social organisations, [are] arenas of struggle . . . riven with actual or potential conflict . . . poorly coordinated . . . ideologically diverse' (p. 19). This negative pitch is balanced by the tenet that recognising diversity as a strength is one of the cultural norms underpinning successful school improvement: 'there is freedom for individuals to realise shared goals in different ways' (Stoll and Fink 1996: 96).

For many teachers this 'freedom' remains often invoked, yet rarely realised. What binds many teams is not a sense of common purpose and liberty to operate as an individual, but a shared masquerade. This is sustained through systematic employment of avoidance: to us, 'potential disruption [outweighs] the benefits of resolution', so, ostrich-like, we bury our collective heads in the sand (Morgan 1987: 205–7). What we want to do is tend our gardens, our way. The garden walls are comforting: they are built of the closed door of the classroom, the administrative focus of meetings. Different ways take precedence over shared goals.

The alternatives to copeability are equally destructive. Teams can be torn apart or fragmented by their failure to recognise the complexities of their project and their constituent selves.

In selves

For the constituent selves in a team are nothing if not complex. Like any profession, teaching has its own set of platitudes, of seasoned clichés dusted off and uttered almost in unison at appropriate moments. To the newly-qualified: *don't smile until Christmas*. To the overworked: *why don't you take a night off?* To the interviewee: *this is about finding out if they're right for you as much as if you're right for them*. The one piece of counsel I have neither received, offered, nor heard offered is: *just be yourself*.

For, at work, we are not ourselves. Each day is crammed with role-play. In our interactions with students we act many parts: nice cop, nasty cop, well of infinite patience, hound on a short leash, possessor of indefatigable sense of humour, and so on. These roles form our repertoire as professionals: we accumulate the scripts over years of experience and deftly switch between them as the need arises. Part of supporting colleagues with students is picking up on the script or strategy they are employing. It is normal for teachers to shout one minute and smile the next, to growl and giggle almost simultaneously.

These 'strategies' are employed because they have a certain functional efficiency: they get results from students. Yet they have a further function: they serve to maintain a protective distance between our professional and personal selves. We all know when the veneer is thin: when we are tired, when the membrane between work and home is weakened. At such moments we become vulnerable. Every teacher has a story of a time when they 'really' lost their temper or have 'really' been upset – often a time when a student's comment or behaviour has penetrated the defences and tellingly 'struck home'.

Similarly, in our relationships with colleagues we operate in different roles. Part of the process of evolving a culture as a team or as a staff is working out which bits of our identities we can reveal, and when. We learn to conform. School and team cultures can accommodate a range of mildly non-conformist behaviours, which often become part of the daily cultural landscape.[2] These are certainly signifiers of homogeneity; impenetrable to outsiders and fostered by staff through acceptance of idiosyncrasy and respect for seemingly arbitrary conventions. Their sites tend to be collegial areas such as the staff-room or department office. They are humorously present in the staff meeting, the briefing, the leaving speech: they become the public expression of 'our' tolerance, 'our' unity, re-enacted in the presence of and sanctioned by management. Yet they do not signify unity of purpose or shared beliefs.

These recognitions of diversity and difference are *easy*: they promote a view of the school as benevolent, while in reality 'inoculating the public with a contingent evil to prevent or cure an essential one', in Barthes' words (Barthes 1973: 150). The essential 'evil' here is the danger posed by the true nature of teams and of teachers. While we are perfectly able to accept the plural nature of our identities when dealing with students, yet we are not able to do so with our colleagues. We are trapped within fixed notions of our identities as professionals.

Everything about school culture fixes us: from our positions in the school hierarchy to our chair in the staff-room. As we have seen, divergence from script is either soon centripetally accommodated – or serves to relegate us to the status of heretic. There is a set pattern of professional development: one chooses the pastoral 'ladder' or the curriculum 'ladder': one 'moves on' or 'gets stuck'. Attitudinal or competence-based movement within our professional identities is largely conceptualised as linear.

According to Huberman (1992), professional development follows themes of 'survival' and 'discovery' at the entry stage, followed by 'stabilisation', but then the career can go in various ways. 'Activism' may characterise the next stage, or it might be 'self-doubt' and these may be followed by 'serenity' or 'conservation', with the final stage characterised as 'disengagement' – in either 'serene' or 'bitter' versions.

There does seem to be some truth to such conceptualisations. Yet roles are too readily and permanently assumed, prophecies fulfilled, trenches dug. To take an extreme: once teachers 'disengage', the landscape of their daily experience is peopled by managers whom they do not trust and colleagues with whom they do not share their private self, contoured by endless inclines of curriculum and administrative demands, shaped by a history of faddish initiatives and failed reforms and coloured by anger, indignation and reactance. Perhaps they are heretics because they feel entrenched in practices not valued by the hegemonic culture. Perhaps they will not perform the rites of the orthodox not because they disagree with them, but because they feel they simply cannot. Stuck in learned helplessness, they blame everyone for their problems but themselves, because that self is too vulnerable. The cluster of complainers in every school *need* each other: their rhetoric is essentially phatic and reassuring, their constant withdrawal from orthodoxy a desperate bid to stay in the only team they feel able to join. Even within the hegemonic culture change hurts: Fullan remarks that teachers exist in a situation of 'fixity and a welter of forces', and that 'all real change involves loss, anxiety, and struggle' (Fullan 1991: 35). How can those on the edge, without the support of shared orthodox identity, cope with such feelings? Reactance is displaced anxiety: the strong can endure the hurt of change with their eyes fixed on the prize, but for the vulnerable identities of the still-wounded or weak the potential pain is just too much to bear.

While systemic issues such as lack of collegiality and shared goals may have initiated the progress of polarisation, attitudes on both 'sides' become intrinsic to identity. Tellingly, reactance tends to produce equal patterns of dominance in management. It seems that no amount of proaction by management can handle the reactors, and as school organisations slowly shift into postmodern shapes, it must be remembered that for every teacher who is recruited into hegemonic practices, there are some left behind, choosing or being forced into oppositional identities. In the rhetoric of Armageddon, it appears that for some the end will be forever nigh.

Yet on reflection it seems evident that movement between Huberman's 'themes' is not linear or progressive. Teachers seem to shift *modally* between these descriptors day by day, lesson by lesson, initiative by initiative. All teachers, surely, survive, control, secure, analyse and innovate at various times: similarly, all teachers disengage. The factors which determine both mode and its duration must be *social*.

To return to my Monday:

> By Lesson Five I need help. Help comes in the shape of Year 10. As luck would have it, we are due to study a poem about identity. I ask them to help me make a list of all the different people I am. My list looks something like this:

At work
- teacher with difficult class
- teacher with nice class
- teacher when Headteacher is in classroom
- teacher with upset pupil
- teacher with nasty pupil
- teacher having joke in corridor

Elsewhere
- husband
- son
- acquaintance

- friend
- mate
- customer (shaven and smart)

- Head of Department (in meeting with Headteacher)
- HoD (in meeting with team)
- HoD (being sympathetic)
- HoD (telling off)
- HoD having go at someone else's class
- HoD talking to parents
- HoD being creative
- HoD doing paperwork

- customer (unshaven and scruffy
- bloke on Tube
- occasional broadcaster
- musician
- student

- bloke in pub
- cook
- handyman (ha ha)

They then do their own lists for themselves. While they write, one pupil asks me, 'How do we do it, sir? How do we change from one to the other?' Another replies: 'It all depends on who you're with.' I say, 'Pupils who get in trouble are the ones who cannot shift from *street kid* to *obedient pupil*.' A girl says, 'And teachers who get in trouble are the ones who can't shift from *bloke in pub* to *teacher when Headteacher is in classroom*.' We laugh. Someone says, 'It's sad, though, isn't it? We can't ever be ourselves.' The girl replies, 'Yes, but it's about surviving.'

What can we learn from thirty-one people contemplating the post-modern abyss on a Monday afternoon in Sutton? It appears that these students are acutely aware of the complexities of their own being: they are aware of the plural nature of identity, aware of the social con-struction of these identities, aware of their own positioning within discourses – and of the consequences of mismatch. There is a sense of unease here, a sense of loss of a unitary self that might be dismissable as premature *weltschmirtz* or teenage angst were it not so resonant. These students have, after all, rescued one teacher from 'disengage-ment' and flipped him neatly over into a positive mode. And finally, there is the pragmatism of the girl's final statement: *it's about surviving*. She understands the idea that lies at the core of this chapter: that of *repertoire*.

Repertoire

> The word is always partly someone else's. (Mikhail Bakhtin)

The teaching profession specialises in metaphors of performance. Our development plans have *performance indicators*. Teacher-training pro-grammes have *performance profiles*. Here in the UK, at the time of writing, we are facing the introduction of *performance-related pay* and *performance thresholds*. Teachers express the pressures of complex daily professional lives in terms of *juggling* or *plate-spinning*. We talk of teaching students to *jump through hoops* so they can *perform* better in examinations. It is my contention in this chapter that this dead metaphor needs re-invigorating in order for us to reach a new, constructive understanding of the nature of the work of teachers and students.

Actors

First, the notion of performance carries an implication of fragmentation, of splitting, of there being a fundamental difference between 'self' and 'action'. Teachers and students may therefore not be seen as unitary selves, operating as individual identities, but as *actors* with a repertoire of roles which operate concurrently.

Script

Second, performance implies *script*. Each performative act – examination, lesson, dialogue – is predicated upon at least one script or set of discursive rules. These scripts are socially constructed: communication takes place within a pattern of existing social relationships. The meanings we create are always relative; people actively take on specific scripts or discourses through which they shape the world and are shaped by it. Our 'selves', our 'own voices' are contingent upon the social groups and practices we have been brought up in. As Bakhtin (1981) put it, the word is always partly someone else's: we cannot use a word, a gesture, a phrase, a text without it already having a socially-constructed value or inflection.

Repertoire-building

The implications for schooling are manifold. The learning process is one of enculturation, or of *repertoire-building*. That there can be no unitary notion of the curriculum is the most significant: it is more helpful to consider the school as a site in which multiple scripts co-exist, each with specific purposes and contexts in which they are used, and each with equal value. The originators of such scripts or discourses are multi-fold, shifting, dialogic and themselves the sites of competing discourses: government organisations, academic histories of subject specialisms, examination boards, governing bodies, senior management teams, school cultures, departmental cultures, classroom cultures.

To be functionally literate in music is very different from being functionally literate in mathematics. Moreover, each academic subject has its own practices and patterns of social and literate interaction, its own modes of enquiry, its own vocabulary, its own 'grammar', its own rhetoric. To be able to think like a scientist the student needs to be enculturated into the literate practices of scientists. Teachers and students draw upon a repertoire of scripts or discourses, cued by or chosen to suit the contextual subject or interaction. Degrees of success as teachers or learners are determined by the extent to which the script has been adhered to – or the extent to which improvisatory moves fit within acceptable discursive paradigms. Students do not wake up one morning suddenly able to frame hypotheses, link cause and effect, balance opposing points of view, draw conclusions and jump through all the other verbal hoops expected of them. An effective curriculum, then, must comprise deconstructing and constructing the high-status academic discourses that not only bear the stamp of 'success' but also contain within them the key cognitive and metacognitive processes that make each subject make sense.[3]

For teachers, this is a liberating notion. We need to abandon any simplistic sense of fostering 'ownership' of learning, as it too often results in pitching work in students' existing competencies. This 'put it in your own words' pedagogy denies the idea of education as enculturation. Rather, we need to direct our practice openly at expanding repertoires, at teaching the scripts, at seeing each student not as an owner, but as many owners. This allows teachers to pitch high and scaffold, not dumb down and hope for the best. This allows teachers to be *specialists*, to teach their subject in all its complexity.

Rehearsal

Thus, each lesson becomes a *rehearsal*. Students rehearse their roles, construct their scripts as scientists, as geographers, as literary critics. While there are overlaps between these discourses, it is self-defeating to attempt to unify the curriculum, to impose an integrity or homogeneity where there simply is none. It is my experience that once a team sees its project in these terms, the payoff is immediate. The overall pitch of lessons rises. We find ourselves shifting units of work lower and lower down the school. Recently one of my current colleagues found herself teaching exactly the same ideas and material to a Y7 class one lesson, then to a Y12 class the next.

Improvisation

What are the implications of this for teacher–teacher relationships and personal/professional development? What must first be abandoned is any notion of *fixity*. Due to the inherent uncertainties and anxieties of teachers' professional lives, the tendency is to secure things, to write things down. We want procedures. We want rules. We want our schemes of work written down. Yet all of these produce cultures of control, not cultures of learning. All of these contribute to the idea of learning, of teaching, of *being* in a school as static, rather than dynamic: ventriloquy.

It is my experience that most teachers want to be set free from this fixity. The last two department teams I have worked in have taken the plunge. The starting point in each case was a simple exercise in double-loop thinking: given that what we do must be seen as a process of enculturation, what do we like about what we do and what do want to change?[4] Let us see what we do as emergent, not static. Let us see our curriculum as organic: let's write our schemes of work *up*, not write them *down*. Just as students rehearse, take chances, expand their repertoires, let's see what we do every day as rehearsal, as risk-taking, as experimentation with our own repertoires. Let's allow movement, in the curriculum, in the team, in class, in ourselves.

These teams have improvised together. Once broad teaching and learning objectives have been set together, we have worked together on evolving practices that meet those goals. Old hands work with new hands and both benefit from joint experimentation, joint authorship.[5] We have instant access to each other's repertoires. We add to and refine our own stock of scripts and become adept at improvising. What this process has instilled in these teams is a sense of all members, regardless of status, as being first and foremost creative teachers united – made integral – by a common project: let's make what we do the best we possibly can. It allows us to have setbacks, to admit our differences and weaknesses: when the overarching aim is to learn together and when the natural pitch of conversation is about what we do in class there is room for us all to be strong, to be vulnerable, to be moving, to be stuck. We are allowed to be positive, allowed to be negative, allowed to be heretics, allowed to be believers, for none of these is seen as definitive of *who* we are. Perhaps the only constant is a constructive 'instability that [will] help a new pattern of behaviour [emerge]' (Morgan 1997: 269). Above all, it allows us to cope with the sea of internal and external narratives: we are all experts, all just beginning.

Delivery and modality

The solution therefore may be a rediscovery of senses 1 and 2 of *deliver*: 'set free' and 'assist at birth of; give birth to'. Freed from fixity and seeing our aim as being to allow for, add to and develop our own repertoires and those of our students, *delivery* should entail a recognition of integrity in the teacher, the team and the student as emergent rather than given; of each constituent as a part of, not apart from, the whole: a recognition that the processes of *being* in a school, in a team, in a class, in a 'self' are stative rather than static; modular rather than linear. Such a shift in thinking entails understanding and allowance of the multiplicity and flux of the self at all levels, from the composition and 'management' of teams as achieving fluency through fluidity, to teachers' attitudes to learners.

The question is this: if we see school, team and classroom methods and systems as fluid rather than fixed, how will that help us become better, more fulfilled teachers? Don't we need the secure anchors of rigid procedures, rigid notions of right and not-right, rigid concepts of self and other?

It is indeed a risky business for a teacher or manager, this loosening of the bonds. Yet how can we realistically survive – and work effectively – if we try to preserve anachronistic ideas about our jobs, our colleagues and ourselves? As a child I was terrified on my first flight when I saw the wings wobble: once someone had explained that rigid wings would cause the jet to shake itself to pieces I gave silent thanks for their flexibility. So it is for the adult me, the teacher and teamleader: a self and a structure that are too rigid will shake themselves to pieces in the flux of my daily professional life. By accepting the constancy of change I can cope with it. By accepting that my job is a sea of stories I can navigate it.

At the end of a lesson, a Year 11 pupil said to me, 'You make it seem as if all this stuff about the novel is coming from us, but really you've got it all written down in your planning book, haven't you?' I smiled and closed my planner, so that he could not see that my notes for that lesson consisted of one word: *onwards*.

Notes

1 Scott (1990) describes antihegemonic cultural practice as 'the hidden transcript' and argues that it is located in sites that fulfil certain criteria:

> The social sites of the hidden transcript are those locations in which the unspoken riposte, stifled anger, and bitten tongues created by

relations of domination find a vehement, full-throated expression. It follows that the hidden transcript will be least inhibited when two conditions are fulfilled: first, when it is voiced in a sequestered social site where the control, surveillance, and repression of the dominant are least able to reach, and second, when this sequestered social milieu is composed entirely of close confidants who share similar experiences of domination. (p. 120)

Common sites of the 'hidden transcript' in schools are the car-park, the smokers' room, etc.

2 Stoll and Fink (1996) describe the presence in schools of 'metaphor, customs, rituals, ceremonies, myths, symbols, stories and humour' (p. 82).

3 For an overview of research into and theories of the social construction of literacy and schools as sites of multiple literacies, see Lankshear (1997).

4 Morgan 1997: 83–90. Single-loop learning is characterised by an organisation's inability to think beyond its habitual processes and conceptual models despite the demands placed on it and its own requirements – rather like our department had been previously. Double-loop learning occurs when an organisation questions whether its habitual processes and conceptual models are appropriate and has the ability to change these paradigms and practices accordingly. See also Stoll and Fink (1996) on 'stuck' and 'moving' schools (pp. 32–3, 89).

5 See Little (1990) pp. 168–71 for an exploration of what 'veteran teachers' can gain from close colleagues.

References

Bakhtin, M. (1981) *The Dialogic Imagination: Four Essays by Bakhtin*, (tr. C. Emerson and M. Holquist), Austin TX: Texas University Press.

Ball, S. (1990) *The Micro-politics of the School*, London: Routledge.

Barthes, R. (1973) *Mythologies* (tr. A. Lavers) St. Albans: Granada.

Darling-Hammond, L. (1990) 'Teacher professionalism: why and how?' in A. Lieberman (ed.) *Schools as Collaborative Cultures: The Future Now*, Basingstoke: Falmer Press.

Fullan, M. (1991) *The New Meaning of Educational Change*, London: Cassell.

Huberman, A. (1992) 'Teacher development and instructional mastery' in A. Hargreaves and M. Fullan (eds) *Understanding Teacher Development*, London: Cassell.

Lankshear, C. (1997) *Changing Literacies*, Buckingham: Open University Press.

Lieberman, A. and Miller, L. (eds) (1991) *Staff Development for Education in the '90s: New Demands, New Realities, New Perspectives*, New York: Teachers College Press.

Little, J. W. (1990) 'Teachers as colleagues' in A. Lieberman (ed.) *Schools as Collaborative Cultures: The Future Now*, Basingstoke: Falmer Press.

Morgan, G. (1997) *Images of Organisation* (second edition), London: Sage.

Rosenholtz, S. (1991) *Teachers' Workplace: The Social Organisation of Schools*, New York: Teachers College Press.

Scott, J. (1990) *Domination and the Arts of Resistance: Hidden Transcripts*, New Haven CN: Yale University Press.

Stoll, L. and Fink, D. (1996) *Changing Our Schools: Linking School Effectiveness and School Improvement*, Buckingham: Open University Press.

7   Schools as places of learning and integrity

Caroline Lodge

The sense of increasing complexity and uncertainty which marked the twentieth century was captured by the poet Yeats when he used the phrase 'Mere anarchy is loosed upon the world'. It can refer to the human destruction inflicted on peoples and the environment as well as the multiplying communications media. In the developed world the century saw the creation of lifestyles and living conditions unimaginable and impossible at any earlier period of history. Old certainties were challenged so that the only certainty remaining was that the pace and complexity of this change would continue. This postmodern condition 'of ephemerality, fragmentation, discontinuity and the chaotic' (Harvey 1990: 44) has implications and potential for integrity in schools as organisations, and is the subject matter of this chapter.

Schools experience these changes to the world in two ways. First, change impacts upon the business of school, the learning of the young people: inevitably the integrity of the school, in both the senses used in this book (of wholeness and of moral uprightness), is challenged. Second, schools are located in communities who also experience the impact of these changes in their families, work, homes, leisure activities and their communications with others.

When we explore the impact on and possibilities for the schools as organisations we are confronted with a problem. We must draw on language available to us, which is redolent of current concepts, making it hard to find the language to describe something which is unfamiliar. The language of school organisation is of structures, staff, policies, processes, boundaries and budgets. These are some of the concrete aspects of organisation. While they are significant, to focus on these aspects of organisation does not reveal the connections between them. It is in the connections that we will find integrity. We need to find new ways to describe new concepts. Metaphors are a powerful way of developing new understandings about organisations (Morgan 1986) and so we need new metaphors and linguistic tools to see organisations in new ways.

The world of art provides new ways of looking at familiar things. The 'house' of the Turner Prize winner, Rachel Whiteread, was a challenge to conceptualisation of a complex but familiar construction. This sculpture made insubstantial the structural features of the house (walls, window frames and so forth) by representing them as absences. It made concrete what we experience as space. The artist invited us to conceive everyday objects in a new way and provoke new perceptions by making concrete the spaces and giving substance to the insubstantial.

Whiteread shows us what is not concrete. To consider the integrity of school organisations we need to look at what connects schools as organisation, the relationships between people, the activities which connect the people to the purpose of the organisation, the negotiation of differences between roles, hierarchies and positioning in relation to boundaries. To consider integrity in the sense of wholeness we need to consider more than the separate parts. Integrity will be found in the interconnections between the parts, and their combined contribution to the organisation.

This chapter considers integrity in school organisations in three sections:

• schools, change and complexity;
• responses in schools to these conditions; and
• the possibilities for integrity in schools.

Schools, change and complexity

Individuals, and the organisations of which they are members, have to cope with continual change. Complexity and disconnection are experienced in the separate, conflicting and unequal parts of the organisation as well as in the pattern of connections between them. This pattern of connections between its members gives form to the organisation, to its structures, processes and strategies. The complexity has to be embraced by the organisation in order that the purposes of the organisation remain connected to the individual's purposes in belonging to it. Absenteeism by students and their disaffection can be indicators of a serious problem – young people do not feel connected to the school or its purposes. And in some schools, this is also true of some of the adults.

Each individual brings to the organisation experiences which constantly challenge their idea of themselves as an individual. This has become much more complex as old certainties about gender, ethnicity, class and adulthood have been swept away. Understanding ourselves as workers is increasingly problematic as patterns of employment and unemployment are changing, and permanent unemployment may be part of our social landscape for many years to come (Fink 1998).

Freire has spoken of each person's 'ontological vocation to be more fully human' (Freire 1990: 55). The business of schools is, in part, to help young people work out the meaning of this vocation but social issues are rarely unproblematic. Schools are particularly vulnerable as sites where socially contested ideas are played out. An example of social issues affecting schools is the perceived under-achievement of boys. The problem is conceived by policy-makers, in part, as one of an attractive but anti-achieving 'laddish' culture. Schools are required to provide an antidote, partly because the wider society is seen as less amenable to change and therefore cannot provide the solution (Epstein *et al.* 1998).

Each individual brings their own sense of self, along with all its inherent conflicts and contradictions, the complexity of their multiple interrelationships, their different sense of the purpose of the school. The teachers bring moral purpose (Fullan and Hargreaves 1992), the need to earn a living, the need to establish meaning through work and a set of beliefs and values which may or may not conflict with those of the school. Young people bring their own purposes, including social identity and development, ambitions, resistance. The organisation of the school has to allow this plurality of human experience to be made available to the young people, which is especially challenging if the school is to avoid both chaos and dogma.

Reflecting the increasing trend towards complexity in society, schools have more goals, more complex goals and less time to meet them (Creemers 1996). Our schools prepare youngsters for a world which no longer exists. An American analysis broadly fits the UK history, and uses a series of metaphors (Schlechty 1990). In the past schools were required to function as a kind of community church, promoting morality, civic good and reverence for school, while teaching was regarded as a sacred profession. In the later industrial period schools retained their moral purpose but became more like factories whose function was selection, grading and standardisation for economic purposes. They were managed according to principles derived from a view of the organisation as a machine and teachers were regarded as skilled technocrats. In addition to their 'church' and 'factory' functions schools in the post-war period also became like hospitals. From this time their function was also to heal the injustices of industrial society. Schools today have adapted and embrace aspects of all three functions, despite the contradictions and tensions which the varying functions bring. They face a future function, which Schlechty describes without metaphor. Now and in the future schools must also be *knowledge-work organisations*, to help students learn what they need to know in a knowledge-work world.

While all organisations face increasing complexity, schools have an additional difficulty because an important additional function is to prepare young people for a world not yet known. A challenge for schools is that they are simultaneously concerned with meeting a range of goals in the present complex circumstances and preparing young people for the unknown and unknowable complexity of the future.

Such potential disconnection between purposes, or uncertainty about the place and role of the individual in the world, has in the past been resolved or removed by authoritarian decisions, operating through class, gender, ethnicity and other divisions. The established conventions of power are no longer as acceptable, and this too is having an impact on schools. Until recently most power in the school was held by one person, usually a white, lower-middle class male (Grace 1995). The headmaster could speak proprietorially of 'my school' and could exercise autocratic power over the curriculum, staffing appointments and promotions, rules, policies and so forth with little account taken of the views or experience of any other members of the school. This has changed. Governors now hold many of those powers, and others have been taken by the government or by parents. Within schools there are complexities in the power relationships: between different hierarchies and groups of teachers and other staff, between the students and the adults, and these have effects on learning. Influence and power over schools is also located externally, for example with policy makers, OFSTED, parents and press.

We now turn to the responses that these pressures may produce in schools.

Responses to the postmodern condition

This section considers responses by schools to the ambiguity and complexity of the postmodern world and suggests that many are short-term rather than sustainable. In many cases these responses are likely to inhibit learning, the school's principal purpose. There are two sources for these responses: schools' external context and their internal conditions.

According to Foucault, if organisations are to thrive in the postmodern context they need to embrace 'what is positive and multiple, difference over uniformity, flows over unities, mobile arrangements over systems' (quoted in Harvey 1990: 44). Educational policy in the UK embodies none of these recommended features. It has shown an 'obsession with failure' (Mortimore 1996), embodied in an examination system which selects and sorts pupils and an inspection system which does the same for schools. Instead of the multiple, policy-makers recommend simple and singular instrumental solutions such as the 'one size fits all' National Curriculum or the Literacy Hour. Difference and experimentation are discouraged, compliance is enforced through OFSTED inspections, LEAs' Education Development Plans and standards for teachers. Change is controlled through episodic policy announcements (currently a new initiative is launched about every six weeks), while structural solutions are favoured over local communities developing responses of their choice.

These features of policy promote short-termism and instrumentalism which in turn can push the school towards particular responses. The linked consequences for schools may be described as follows.

1   *The purpose of schooling is inverted.* The students are pressured into performing well in order to enhance the reputation of the school. The focus of the school is on student performance. However, a focus on performance is likely to depress performance, while a focus on learning will promote learning and performance (Entwistle 1987; Dweck and Leggett, 1988).

2   *Problems are presented as solutions.* The 'obsession with leadership' (Reynolds 1998) by UK policy-makers, draws on the attraction of strong, heroic leadership in turbulent times and on the romantic and prevalent notion that leadership is '*the* causal entity rendering ill-structured, complex problems meaningful and explicable' (Gronn 1996). But this individualisation is experienced by headteachers as perilous and isolating. It is a favoured policy to introduce a super-hero to a school with multiple and complex problems. Any failure can be blamed on the super-hero and leave policy and policy-makers unscathed. The schools in these circumstances are no better off, as we have seen with the policy to close some schools and to reopen them as Fresh Start schools.

3   *Expectations about the pace of change produce conflict.* Policy-makers' time does not synchronise with schools', teachers' or learners' time (Cuban 1995). Policy-makers want immediate outcomes from initiatives, but change at the level of culture of the

school, organisational learning, teachers' practice and young people's learning takes time and is rarely unproblematic.

4 *Policy contradictions are experienced at school level.* For example, an examination system which selects and sorts pupils is inconsistent with other policy attempts to raise education standards for all (Robinson 1997). Social inclusion policy is experienced as in conflict with the drive to raise school performance levels. Some of these tensions arise from the fundamentalism of prescribed strategies, based on unquestioned beliefs and dogmas and not on knowledge, research or on values which honour people. (The policy of 'naming and shaming' 'failing' schools is a case in point.)

5 *Schools become separated from their environments.* As local differences are devalued and singular prescriptions are enforced, teaching strategies take less account of what learners bring to the situation in terms of previous knowledge, beliefs about learning, learning strategies and so on. There is an emphasis on coverage and performance, rather than on learning.

6 *Schools provide fragmented and unconnected experiences for young people.* Curriculum is organised around knowledge categorisation rather than human development. Important aspects of children's development such as the social aspects of young people's lives are ignored in this curriculum. Little account is taken of what young people themselves might have to say about their own learning needs.

7 *The complex is represented as simplistic.* Definitions of success are limited to a narrow range of outputs such as the proportion of pupils attaining higher grades in five GCSE subjects, which do not reflect the more complex and human purposes of schooling.

8 *Schools become exclusive.* A section of students (borderline C/D grades at GCSE) is given higher value than others. Those who need extra resources or help to achieve the standardised averages (young people who have limited use of English language, refugees, pupils with physical or learning disabilities, students who cause the school difficulties) are devalued. A narrow range of teaching styles such as 'chalk and talk, drill and recite' still dominates the repertoire of most teachers despite its poor track record (Joyce *et al.* 1997).

9 *Activity is presented as taking charge.* According to Senge (1990), a significant organisational learning disability is the illusion of taking charge, through claimed proactivity which is in fact reactivity in disguise. Management activity focuses on the processes of planning and target setting which replaces concerns for the outcomes of such processes.

These responses mean that important aspects of what it means to be 'at school' have been de-selected. Schools feel they are unable to explore and experiment with their curriculum (both the content and form of what is taught). They ignore what it means to be a human in our school system either as an adult working under intensified conditions, or as a young person exploring their development as a social, physical, political, learning human. It is based on a mistaken assumption that there is a direct or linear connection between policy mandates and children's learning (McLaughlin 1990).

The nine conditions resulting from external pressures become accepted by many within the system as the way things have to be. They exist alongside internal conditions which also make it hard for schools to be adaptive. Salary structures and management hierarchies are hard to shift, new skills hard to acquire, new technology expensive and quickly out of date. As a result we find that conditions within schools may result in three further conditions which challenge integrity:

10 *Energy and attention are consumed by the immediate and the day to day as a result of intensification of teachers' work.* Teachers have lost control of the pattern of their work as well as any view of the future of schooling (Apple 1983). Time is the resource which is most lacking in schools, and not just time for lessons, but for reflection, exploration, speculation and socialisation. Students are increasingly experiencing the pressures of school in the same ways.

11 *Stakeholders avoid risks.* Teachers, parents and governors reproduce their own experience of schooling, perpetuating systems and features of their own formal education.

12 *Conventional beliefs and concepts about learning and classrooms persist.* These have a powerful influence on teaching, assessment and conditions for learning. Classrooms show remarkable similarity all over the world in their form, structure, appearance and processes, and are resistant to change, especially to technological change (Cuban 1993).

These twelve organisational conditions are responses to difficult circumstances, but they all threaten integrity, both in the sense of wholeness and also in relation to the moral value of schooling.

Organisations with integrity

So far this chapter has explored the ever-changing context of schools and considered how their responses to change are often conditioned by a combination of pressures from the external world and forces within the organisation itself. These responses often lack integrity. We should not wonder that it is hard to recruit people to work as teachers, and that many youngsters are disenchanted with the education on offer and respond with disappointment, disengagement and disappearance (Barber 1996). School organisations can be more satisfying work places for adults as well as young people, where the organisation is responsive to and benefits from the shifting context, and the learning of the young people can be enhanced. The final section of this chapter explores these possibilities for schools.

Conceptions of schools, as other organisations, are imbued with notions of Newtonian physics, and the language usually used to describe them derives from images of the organisation as machine. The machine metaphor allows us to consider the constituent parts of the whole, and then to make mechanical adjustments or to rebuild the whole from its constituent parts. The structures are seen as solid, bounded and functioning independently in predetermined sequences to produce a desired outcome. The whole organisation is bounded, controlled by operatives and by and large continues to function whatever its environment. Much school effectiveness literature and government policy draws on the metaphor of the school as machine.

As in physics, new understandings have challenged Newtonian concepts in the study of organisations. To ensure that schools have integrity in their organisation, we need to approach schools less as mechanics concerned with the constituent parts, the structures, the processes, the curriculum subjects. We need to learn from quantum physicists and explore the connections and separations in schools processes and the people of the community.

New ways of thinking about organisations have been developed in response to increasing complexity and flexibility. A few examples demonstrate this. *Leadership and the New Science* explicitly takes the metaphors of new science as a starting point for the study of organisations (Wheatley, 1992). Drawing also on lessons from both biology and physics, Garmston and Wellman (1995) suggest that schools need to be more adaptive. They argue that quantum physics has enabled us to conceptualise our world in new ways. It can be studied as energy rather than just as observable substance. Attention needs to be paid to schools' flows and interchange of energy.

Senge's creative ideas about learning organisations are widely found in business as well as educational literature (Senge 1990). Within education ideas influenced by new thinking include the 'butterflies' from Birmingham, which are 'small interventions or punctuations which have a disproportionate effect on meaning and change' and are derived from chaos theory (Brighouse and Woods 1999: 109). An example of re-conceptualising the school can be found in *The Intelligent School* (MacGilchrist *et al.* 1997). As the title suggests, the authors use the metaphor of the school as a brain. They draw on Gardner's theory of multiple intelligences (Gardner 1984) and describe a range of intelligences which the school needs. Teachers find this attractive, possibly because it offers a new and creative way of conceptualising the school and relationships between its functions, purposes and activities.

From these different perspectives we can begin to offer some themes which can be pursued in a school with integrity.

First, *the learning of young people at best connects all aspects of the school organisation.* Schools exist in order to promote children's learning. Effective learning involves processes such as these:

- making connections about what has been learned in different contexts;
- exploring how the learning contexts have played a part in making the learning effective;
- engaging with others in learning;
- reflecting about one's own learning and learning strategies; and
- setting further learning goals (Watkins *et al.* 1996).

Organisational arrangements can either block each of these processes or they can facilitate and encourage them. All these processes are necessary for the learning of the individual, of whatever age, as well as for organisational learning. They can all be enhanced by interaction with others. In a school these processes are promoted through active and collaborative learning, the learner taking responsibility for and learning about their own learning. Given the uncertainty of their future and the need for adaptability, young people are helped to develop the ability to monitor, reflect upon and review their own learning (Watkins *et al.* 2000). The school's general discourse about learning reinforces and promotes these processes at an organisational level.

Second, *the school takes account of young people's experiences and the conditions of their learning* (Sarason 1990; Ruddock *et al.* 1996). One of the tasks for young people is to understand themselves in relation to others. This understanding of the self has become more complex through a multiplicity of media so that the individual identity develops ever-changing possibilities and difficulties. Romantic and modernist notions of the self crumble in the face of the saturation of interrelations which each individual experiences (Gergen 1991). Globalisation effects our relationships with other people by concentrating time and place so that events which take place in apparently distant parts of the world can immediately have effects on our lives (Giddens 1998).

The curriculum of a school with integrity takes as its starting point the lives of the learners. It is based on an extended and continuous dialogue with students about what it means to be a learner, about learning, about why some kinds of knowledge are valued, about the difficult and unanswerable problems of being human. This dialogue is continuous and engages and enriches all members of the school community (Rudduck *et al.* 1996; Pickering 1997; Fielding 1999).

Third, in the school with integrity *new technologies invite new forms of communication and connection between the learner and other people.* They also develop new ways of manipulating information, facilitating collaboration and changing teachers' roles so that they monitor, direct and assist learners. Our understanding of knowledge and of the potential of the technology to use the plethora of information will profoundly affect the teacher and the learner (Noss and Pachler 1999). It is, for example, challenging the boundaries between these roles in the classroom where the young have more experience of computers than their 'teachers'. Unexamined assumptions have been made about the ways in which children can access information and learn, and about what it is important for them to learn, and about what is necessary to prepare them for their future life. These areas are not given attention by the dominant discourse and are treated as if they are unproblematic. For example, at the most reductionist, ICT skills are being promoted as necessary to access the expanding volume of information. But ownership of the clock radio, referred to in the first chapter, is not enough. In the school with integrity active learners will go beyond access. They learn to develop the ability to evaluate, analyse and interpret information, to make meaning from it and connections with previous learning and thereby to turn information into their knowledge.

Fourth, *integrity, in both the senses used in this book, depends in the school upon relationships.* This includes those relationships which extend beyond its physical boundaries – making real the African saying 'it takes a whole village to educate a child'. In 'oldspeak' we referred to structures, the hierarchical arrangements of teachers, organised into cells of subject (secondary schools) or age range (primary schools or key stages). Thinking in this way emphasises chains of command and control. A more visionary and integrative approach views organisation as the connections and relationships between various organisational dimensions which may include curriculum areas, staff groups, or policies and plans. In a book which explored changing the boundaries of learning, Bentley wrote

> We are moving away from the view that learning takes place only inside people's heads, or inside single institutions made for that purpose. The reality is much more complex and unpredictable – initially more threatening and riskier, but also potentially far richer and more rewarding.
>
> (Bentley 1998: 157)

Fifth, *roles are treated as flexible*. Being trapped in organisational roles can be one of the main blocks to developing learning organisations (Senge 1990). While nurturing the specific skills and contribution of those who are trained and employed as teachers, the school with integrity regards all school members as learners and welcomes the contribution of other adults and of the students to learning and pedagogy. This lack of rigid adherence to role goes beyond the sharing of the roles of teacher and learner. It embraces changing perceptions of these roles and others. Experimentation with job titles already takes place and this is an indication of how perceptions of roles are changing. Lack of rigidity in role functions encourages responsiveness to the context and to working in different combinations to enhance the learning of young people. This flexibility also allows organisations to make much more of their resources of human capabilities: students who are also teachers, and teachers who see themselves as learners.

Other accepted and standard arrangements such as the school day (MacBeath, this volume), pupil groupings or the physical arrangements of school can be questioned. Technological developments present the possibility of access to a huge range of information from many different sites at any time. Schools may not need to depend on rigid groupings, regular and simultaneous timings and to demand the physical presence of learners or teachers as they currently do. This is not to argue that schools will only exist in virtual reality because schooling's function is by no means limited to providing information. Learning is often more effective in collaborative settings (Watkins *et al.* 1996), and young people need and enjoy the social development which schools can provide.

Sixth, there is an explicitness in handling tensions in the organisation.

> The beginning of wisdom is the discovery that there exist contradictions of permanent tension with which it is necessary to live and that it is above all not necessary to seek to resolve.
>
> (Gorz quoted in Ball 1998: 81)

Foucault enjoins us to accept the postmodern condition and 'to develop action, thought, and desires by proliferation, juxtaposition, and disjunction' (quoted in Harvey 1990: 44). Schools need strong connections to their external communities, including support for some of these difficult tensions and relationships. Tensions, dilemmas and paradoxes are the future of organisations and reconciling apparent contradictions is increasingly what managers do (Handy 1994). The ambiguities and contradictions may also imply a challenge to some long assumed hierarchies, boundaries and notions of what a school is. Some have been referred to in the previous section, but we should note other tensions which may not be capable of resolution:

- the purposes of schooling are multiple and at times contradictory;
- schools must meet individual needs within a communal context;
- schools need to provide stability for their members, especially the young, and also be adaptable both for survival and to maximise learning;
- schools need to connect to the external world but filter out damaging influences;
- many forces affecting change are located externally, but integrated change can only be brought about from within the organisation.

Conclusion

A school of integrity is a place where the individual has unique significance, but where the combination of individuals supports the learning of all. The central focus of the school is the learning of the young people, and all the structures are created, adapted and constantly reviewed to keep this purpose in mind. The forms and structures of the organisation depend upon the learner not the curriculum or status hierarchy. The complexity for individuals and the community is recognised. Thus both the structures and the curriculum take account of non-linear patterns and unexpected linkages. Helping young people discover what it means to live and learn in a postmodern world is a central purpose of schooling. Boundaries between different roles (teacher and learner), between the school and its communities, between aspects of the curriculum are permeable.

In his poem *Snow*, Louis MacNeice describes how perceptions of the world can shift and how the view of the garden under snow from the window made him see 'the drunkenness of things being various'. This is an apt metaphor for the future of organisations as is his description of the world as 'incorrigibly plural'. Our schools need to encourage an appreciation of the world, its complexity and possibilities in all its drunken plurality, and of the open-endedness of learning.

References

Apple, M. W. (1983) 'Work, class and teaching' in S. Walker and L. Barton (eds), *Gender, Class and Education*, Lewes: Falmer Press.

Ball, S. J. (1998) 'Educational studies, policy entrepreneurship and social theory' in R. Slee, G. Weiner and S. Tomlinson (eds), *School Effectiveness for Whom? Challenges to the School Effectiveness and School Improvement Movements*, London: Falmer Press.

Barber, M. (1996) *The Learning Game: Arguments for an Education Evolution*, London: Gollancz.

Bentley, T. (1998) *Learning Beyond the Classroom: Education for a Changing World*, London: Routledge.

Brighouse, T. and Woods, D. (1999) *How to Improve Your School*, London: Routledge.

Creemers, B. (1996) 'The goals of school effectiveness and school improvement' in D. Reynolds, R. Bollen, B. Creemers, D. Hopkins, L. Stoll and N. Lagerweij (eds), *Making Good Schools: Linking School Effectiveness and School Improvement*, London: Routledge.

Cuban, L. (1993) 'Computers meet classroom: classroom wins', *Teachers College Record*, 95(2): 185–210.

Cuban, L. (1995) 'The myth of failed school reform', *Education Week*, 1 November.

Dweck, C. and Leggett, E. (1988) 'A social-cognitive approach to motivation and personality' *Psychological Review*, 95(2): 256–73.

Entwistle, N. (1987) *Understanding Classroom Learning*, London: Hodder and Stoughton.

Epstein, D., Elwood, J., Hey, V. and Maw, J. (eds.) (1998) *Failing Boys? Issues in Gender and Achievement*, Buckingham: Open University Press.

Fielding, M. (1999) *Students as Radical Agents of Change: a Three Year Case Study*. Paper presented at annual Conference of British Educational Research Association, University of Sussex, September.

Fink, D. (1998) *Leading with Purpose, Passion and Politics: an Invitation to Success*. Paper presented to annual conference of International Schools, Istanbul, April.

Freire, P. (1990) *Pedagogy of the Oppressed*, London: Penguin Books.

Fullan, M. and Hargreaves, A. (1992) *What's Worth Fighting for in Your School?*, Buckingham: Open University Press.

Gardner, H. (1984) *Frames of Mind: the Theory of Multiple Intelligence*, London: Heinemann.

Garmston, R. and Wellman, B. (1995) 'Adaptive schools in a quantum universe', *Educational Leadership*, (April) 52(7): 6–12.

Gergen, K. J. (1991) *The Saturated Self: Dilemmas of Identity in Contemporary Life*, New York: Basic Books.

Giddens, A. (1998) *The Third Way: the Renewal of Social Democracy*, Cambridge: Polity Press.

Grace, G. (1995) *School Leadership: Beyond Education Management*, London: Falmer Press.

Gronn, P. (1996) 'From transactions to transformations: a new world order in the study of leadership', *Education Management and Administration*, 24(1): 7–30.

Handy, C. (1994) *The Empty Raincoat*, London: Hutchinson.

Harvey, D. (1990) *The Condition of Postmodernity*, Oxford: Blackwell.

Joyce, B., Calhoun, E. and Hopkins, D. (1997) *Models of Learning – Tools for Teaching*, Buckingham: Open University Press.

MacGilchrist, B., Myers, K. and Reed, J. (1997) *The Intelligent School*, London: Paul Chapman.

McLaughlin, M. (1990) 'The Rand change agent study revisited: macro perspectives and micro realities', *Educational Researcher*, 19(9): 11–16.

Morgan, G. (1986) *Images of Organization*, London: Sage.

Mortimore, P. (1996) 'We should inspect our obsession with failure', London: *The Independent*, 25 July, Section Two, p. 17.

Noss, R. and Pachler, N. (1999) 'The challenge of new technologies: doing old things in a new way, or doing new things?' in P. Mortimore (ed.), *Understanding Pedagogy and its Impact on Learning*, London: Paul Chapman.

Pickering, J. (1997) *Involving Pupils*, London: University of London Institute of Education School Improvement Network.

Reynolds, D. (1998) 'The school effectiveness mission has only just begun', *Times Educational Supplement*, 20 February, 20.

Robinson, P. (1997) *Literacy, Numeracy and Economic Performance*, London: London School of Economics Centre for Economic Performance.

Rudduck, J., Chaplain, R. and Wallace, G. (eds.) (1996) *School Improvement: What Can Pupils Tell Us?*, London: David Fulton.

Sarason, S. B. (1990) *The Predictable Failure of Educational Reform*, San Francisco: Jossey-Bass.

Schlechty, P. C. (1990) *Schools for the Twenty-First Century: Leadership Imperatives for School Reform*, San Francisco: Jossey-Bass.

Senge, P. M. (1990) *The Fifth Discipline: the Art and Practice of the Learning Organization*, London: Century Business.

Watkins, C., Carnell, E., Lodge, C., Wagner, P. and Whalley, C. (2000) *Learning about Learning*, London: Routledge.

Watkins, C., Carnell, E., Lodge, C. and Whalley, C. (1996) *Effective Learning*, London: University of London Institute of Education School Improvement Network.

Wheatley, M. (1992) *Leadership and the New Science: Learning about Organization from an Orderly Universe*, San Francisco: Berrett-Koehler.

8 Family relationships, learning and teachers – keeping the connections

Neil Dawson and Brenda McHugh

Please don't tell me any bleeding heart stories; if you can prove to me that your work with this child and her family can increase her reading age by 2.2 years in the next six months then I will be interested.

The job was completed within three months – ahead of schedule. Her reading age improved dramatically once she was able to stop worrying about whether her mother was going to commit suicide. She became able to think about life outside the home. She no longer felt responsible and overwhelmed with panic at the paralysing thought of her mother dying and she could begin to focus on learning tasks. She had worried greatly as to who would care for her and her baby brother, with their mother gone and their father unable to cope. Now her ability to concentrate returned.

The hypothesis of this chapter is that it is only by recognising the 'bleeding heart' stories that schools can hope to help many children improve their performance and increase their achievement. It is not an either/or proposition; concentration on the child's preoccupations and dilemmas is not an excuse for lowering learning expectations. The contention is that both the child's emotional predicament and their academic under-functioning are most effectively dealt with as interconnected parts of a complex whole.

The importance of emotions in the learning experience of each child is now better recognised through a range of scientific studies. During the first three years of life the emotional experience of the infant develops through the sounds and images that are stored and processed in the brain during the formative years of brain development (Chiron *et al.* 1997). The social environment of the child, mediated by the primary caregiver, directly influences the final wiring of the brain circuits that are responsible for the socio-emotional development of the individual. The genetic potential of the child can be realised only as it is enabled within nurturing relationships (Schore 1994, 2000).

In professional experience too, a programme for children and their families designed specifically to provide such a better integrated whole has evolved. Over the last twenty years, working in an Education Unit at a Family Service centre, we have been addressing the child's difficulties in the context of their relationships both at school and at home (Dawson and McHugh 1986a, 1986b, 1987, 1988, 1994). Children with emotional, developmental or behavioural difficulties are referred by their school and attend the unit for up to four mornings a week, together with their parents or caregivers. At least eight hundred children plus even more parents and other family members have been through the programme to date. Our daily experience has taught us much about how relationships in families work and also about how children and families relate to teachers and schools. The practice of this unit is underpinned by principles associated with family systems theory.

A systemic view of the family

Rather than considering an individual's behaviour in isolation, a systemic approach focuses on relationships between people. The intention is to think about behaviour in context and to lay emphasis on the interconnectedness of events. Within families repetitive patterns of interaction, which appear to be mutually reinforcing, develop over time. These patterns become established and help to create the predictability and stability that underpin a particular family's identity (Minuchin, 1974; Cooklin, 1982). To some extent this predictability and stability afford the individual family members a degree of protection as a result of belonging to an established group. However, the task of the family is also to be adaptable in relation to events. The need to adapt may come in relation to events occurring within the family itself, for example, those associated with births, marriages, divorce, deaths etc. Flexibility is also required in respect of external influences such as those arising from social, economic, political or cultural factors. For a family to function well it needs to develop the capacity to maintain a sensitive balance between the need for stability and the requirement to be adaptable. When things don't work so effectively, the balance is often tipped too much towards a need for family stability at the expense of the ability to be flexible in relation to life events.

One of the great advantages of adopting a systemic view of the family is that an interactional way of conceptualising behaviour strongly counteracts the potential for overemphasising individual blame. Thinking about behaviour in the context of relationships is also liberating because it offers the potential for a far wider range of choices about how things might change if they get stuck.

A child who is always late for school may receive constant criticism and possibly school sanctions as well. A systemic approach would look for contextual explanations of the lateness. A common situation that can result in a child being late often involves the child being given too much responsibility for the care of younger siblings at the expense of their own need to get to school. Alternatively, the child may be allowed to stay up too late at night with the result that they find it difficult to wake up in the morning. In each scenario, other people are implicated in the behavioural pattern; the child is doing something in relation to family expectations and habits. Potential solutions follow which focus on how relationships need to change in order that the child can get to school on time. How could the need for the younger siblings to be cared for be redistributed within the family more fairly to allow the responsible child to pay more attention to their own need to get to school? Or, in the second example, what would need to happen for the child to get to bed earlier? Who in the family will take responsibility for taking charge to make sure that the new regime is implemented? What implications would this have for other relationships in the family?

In contrast, if the focus of attention remains solely on the child, the attempted solutions will not take into account the full interactional picture. 'Why don't you buy an alarm clock?', would be an individually based intervention intended to cure the lateness. Without a fuller investigation of such things as, who would buy the alarm clock? Where would the money come from? Who would set the clock? Who would pay attention to it? etc., the attempted solution would be highly likely to be ineffective. Such individual, non-integrated solutions have several basic problems. They are not fair because they invariably lead to the child being blamed when the responsibility should lie in the relationship between the child and their significant family members. Such blaming can lead to the child becoming labelled with the consequences that this has for self-esteem and under-functioning. As importantly, solutions that do not fit the relevant contextual situation of the problem do not usually work. If the child recognises that buying an alarm clock isn't going to work it is an unhelpful suggestion that won't be taken up.

Understanding development from a family systems perspective

When a baby is born a dyadic relationship changes to a three-person system. The fundamental tasks of the family need to change so that the balance between individual, couple and parental activities have to be re-negotiated to accommodate the newcomer. Degrees of closeness and intimacy between the adults also change as the competing needs of the baby have their impact. These are regular life issues familiar to us all. They invariably present some difficulties for many couples starting a family. However, if there is sufficient adaptability in their relationship, the transition to a different stage of the family life cycle will be more or less successful. When things go wrong and the developing family shows signs of stress beyond the norm it is important to try to understand what is preventing a healthy transformation.

If there are unresolved difficulties between the adults prior to the child being born, the realignment of relationships has the potential to be problematic. A common pattern that can develop is one in which the mother forms a close bond with the baby and neither adult has the motivation to address the impact that this is having on their relationship as a couple. As a result, the adults drift further apart and their relationship can become more and more strained. In some situations the competing relational needs start to be played out in increasingly acrimonious ways. The mother's need to provide a strong, protective and nurturing relationship with her baby competes with her need for some individual recovery time; at the same time she is likely to be looking to her partner for physical and emotional support. The father may be having difficulty adjusting to the role of father and be unclear about what position to adopt in relation to his partner and child. He may become resentful because he feels that the baby has usurped his position in the family and angry with his partner for allowing it to happen. When communication between the adults is poor there is frequently a tendency for positions to become fixed, which then starts to organise the way in which the future family functions.

Every baby has a need for a secure nurturing relationship with an adult who can enable it to grow physically and psychologically. Bowlby's work on attachment is crucial in helping us to understand the emotional and psychological tasks of the family during the formative early years of a child's life (Bowlby 1971). Moreover, recent research currently being carried out by Schore (2000) has started to uncover the neuro-biological needs of a baby to experience a close attachment relationship during the first two years of life if it is to develop in a psychologically healthy way. This research has the potential to have a dramatic impact on our thinking about the effect that early family relationships have on a child's emotional and psychological development. If the baby's organically based need to form a close attachment relationship with its principal carer is severely interrupted for some reason it is likely to have a significant impact on the growing child's ability to form secure, anxiety-free relationships.

If, for example, the baby has a serious illness or life-threatening physical condition that necessitates extensive medical interventions, this can affect the way that future family relationships develop. Both parents are likely to be extremely anxious and not able to function in as relaxed or confident a manner towards the baby or indeed, towards each other, as they might otherwise have done. Even when the child recovers it is very common for relationships with the baby to remain more cautious and watchful; if the baby has nearly died it is understandable that the parents would not feel so secure about the robustness of their child. When there are other children in the family, this sort of situation can help to explain differences in how siblings develop or are treated by their parents.

To take things back a generation, the same thing may have happened to one of the parents; they might have similarly been very ill as a baby and experienced their parents as being anxious and extra protective of them as they grew up. In this way one parent would be likely to become a very watchful parent in his or her own right. If the other parent did not have the same style of parenting as their partner it can easily lead to disharmony between them. One may accuse the other of being overprotective whilst the other may believe that their partner is too cold and uncaring. If these differences are not resolved there is a strong likelihood that the child may become an innocent player in relationships with their mother and father that have their origins in events that happened long before they were born.

Relevance to schools of a family systems perspective

So, what has this to do with schools? The above examples illustrate one small but critical area of family development. When children get to school age, the patterns of how they relate to people have already become pretty well established. The transition from home to school becomes another major event in the life of the family. If the early years have been relatively secure, in attachment terms, it is likely that the child will make the moves between home and school relatively successfully. However, it is all too easy to see the potential pitfalls that are likely to make transfer more difficult.

A family systems perspective is useful at all stages of school life as children are continually being affected by, and affecting, key relationships in their lives. Family events and crises happen and influence a child's views or ability to function adequately. When there is violence in the home that children are powerless to stop they can become extremely anxious and unable to concentrate on their task at school. They may become violent themselves as a response to their experiences of how relationships are negotiated. If the violence is between their parents they may feel the need to take sides and seek to protect the most vulnerable adult by challenging the authority of the other. They may become increasingly withdrawn and start to stay at home in a vain attempt to prevent the violence. Many children will display symptoms and behaviours which can be seen as attempts to distract adults' attention from their anger with each other so that they have to stop and pay attention to their child's difficulties. For many children family life is fraught with tensions, with many experiencing their parents divorcing acrimoniously. Strains in relation to continuing contact for the child with the absent parent often follow on from a painful divorce. When this is not negotiated well by the adults the frequent result is distress and emotional turmoil for the child. Many children live in extremely complex family organisations, often following divorce or parental separation. In a stepfamily a child may have the experience of being the youngest member of their original family but the eldest in the new family. They may have only had brothers in one family but have stepbrothers and sisters in their stepfamily. In relation to contact arrangements, they may have to make rapid transitions from one family to another and to learn how to accommodate each family's set of beliefs and behavioural expectations.

Whatever the presenting problem the ability to use a systemic perspective can help to make sense of a child's difficulties that are being played out in the school context. Moreover, having a different perspective should encourage the professionals involved to get together the significant family members so that new solutions that make sense to the child and family can be created collaboratively. In our experience of working with families, it is relatively easy to persuade people to become involved in trying to help a child resolve their difficulties if they can be helped to see the relevance and importance of their contribution. Missing, peripheral or absent fathers are often overlooked by professionals when trying to help a child. This is usually a missed opportunity as such fathers frequently have a major influence on the child's thoughts and attitudes to relationships. Involving significant family members who would not normally feel that it was their position to be called on or who might consider they had nothing to offer can be very successful in breathing new life into apparently intractable situations.

Opening a can of worms

When discussing the impact of family relationships on a child's emotional capacity to manage at school, we find that teachers may say that they are becoming anxious because if they start to think in this way it will be like 'opening a can of worms'. Likewise, the suggestion may be made that such considerations are not within a teacher's role but are more appropriate to social workers. A debate will then start about a teacher's need to know more about the emotional world that children bring to the classroom. On one side of this debate we find the opinion that a teacher should only be in school to teach the curriculum as laid down. On the other side there are those who are curious to find out more and consider it essential for the effective implementation of their teaching responsibilities to try to understand how children's psychological experiences affect their ability to access the whole school curriculum (Dowling and Taylor, 1989). The debate is never about whether the so-called 'can of worms' actually exists, but instead centres on whose responsibility it should be to deal with it. There seems to be an acceptance that there is an essential professional activity to be undertaken, and the concern is about the context in which this professional activity should most appropriately take place.

The staff of the Education Unit have continued to work in the context of education rather than move into the world of 'pure' therapy. They are teachers who have gained additional qualifications in family therapy, with the aim of integrating their therapeutic skills and systemic knowledge with their functions as teacher. One of the principal observations arising from their work has been that parents of children displaying emotional and behavioural difficulties often find it easier to talk to teachers about worries concerning their child. This contrasts with many parents' discomfort when being asked to talk to psychologists, psychiatrists or social workers. There is often a deep-seated stigma and mistrust attached to psychology, psychiatry and social work which does not apply in the same way to teaching. Each profession has its own body of knowledge and expertise but also its own sphere of maximum influence. When problems happen in school this is the domain of the teacher and is recognised as such by parents. So, psychologists, psychiatrists and social workers have a lot of the necessary expertise for opening and dealing with the 'can of worms' but are not in the right context to be most effective. Context, in this sense, does not so much mean the geographical location, rather the professional territory of greatest influence.

Seeing connections between a child's presentation at school and their relational experience and learning at home has been crucial in the attempt to create an integrated intervention approach that reflects the true dimensions of the child's world. Seeing the connections and attempting to help teachers, children and family members see and value them in a similar way is a powerful way of intervening with integrity on the child's behalf. Teachers can make a worthwhile difference if they can be helped to see the school and family integrated whole as a sensitive and logical way of helping children in their care.

The job of being curious about what is really underpinning a child's emotional difficulties, when they manifest themselves at school, should be taken on in the context of school and teaching. Families are frequently more available for help with their children within the context of the teacher–parent relationship. Unfortunately, as yet, most teachers don't have the training and confidence to risk looking inside the complexity of these relationships. Nevertheless, the skills and knowledge are available, and the experience of our teacher/therapists has shown that there can be a creative fusion of the two professional domains. There is enormous potential for the creation of the professional role whose function is embedded in the context of a teacher, child and family relationship.

Examples of when working with the family has been important

The 'can of worms' metaphor does not encourage helpful ways of thinking about families. Indeed it may encourage the common comment when colleagues say that a child would be all right if it wasn't for their 'dreadful family', so that blame for the child's unacceptable behaviour switches from the child on to the family. To be successful in working with parents it is essential to develop a no-blame way of thinking and operating. A family needs to be thought about as a resource from which there is the greatest possibility for bringing about effective change for a child presenting difficulties. The family should not be seen as the cause of the child's difficulties no matter how tempting this might sometimes be. This is not only a pragmatic position adopted to facilitate positive involvement with the family but also one based on a belief that families are organisations that can easily become overwhelmed by problems. When this happens relationship patterns develop which do not always support a child being settled enough in school so that they are free to engage in effective learning. This is illustrated in the example of Miranda.

Miranda was a nine year old girl who had been struggling at school.

She was described as dyslexic and had lost confidence in her ability to survive in class in the face of the disparity between her academic performance and that of her peers. She was crying much of the time and said she didn't want to go to school. No amount of one-to-one reassurance or learning support had made any difference. She had a younger sister, Laura, who was seven years old, and doing well at the same school. When Miranda attended the Education Unit with her mother it became apparent very quickly that a pattern had developed between the two of them which maintained Miranda very much in the 'baby' mode of behaviour. Her mother would talk for Miranda and would do everything for her; when Miranda made a mistake with her schoolwork, her mother would search for a rubber and erase the error before she had even made a move. This kind of interaction was generalised in virtually all areas of their relationship; Miranda didn't ever put her own coat on or fasten the zip herself. On odd occasions when her sister Laura attended the Unit, the interactions were totally different; Laura spoke up for herself, managed all her schoolwork independently and didn't need her mother to do up her clothes.

It would be easy to castigate Miranda's mother for not helping her to develop a greater degree of independence. It would also be quite straightforward to understand how a protective pattern had become established in the face of Miranda's dyslexia difficulties. However, Miranda's mother was aware of the pitfalls associated with forming an over-dependent relationship with her eldest daughter. Despite her apparent understanding of the situation they were in, she felt powerless to change her behaviour as she felt Miranda would not be able to manage without her help.

The extra pieces of information that actually helped Miranda's mother adjust her part in the relationship concerned Miranda's experiences around the time of the breakdown of her marriage. As the elder of the two girls, Miranda had been most affected by the high level of acrimony that accompanied her parents' separation when she was four. The arguing had been going on for the previous eighteen months and Miranda's mother had retreated from the marital rows by paying most attention to Laura. As a result of this early closeness with her mother, Laura became securely attached and was able to develop into a confident young girl. Secretly however, Miranda's mother had become guilty about her over-concentration on Laura at the expense of Miranda. Consequently, when Miranda started school, her mother did not feel comfortable about letting her go just at the time when she felt that she needed to lavish attention on her daughter as a way of compensating for the harm that she felt had been done to her. The situation was made worse because there were bitter arguments between Miranda's parents about the arrangements that should be made for her to see her father. As a result, the pattern of excess protection evolved and as Miranda started to function in a dependent way, it confirmed for her mother that there was a need for ever more protection. Once she was able to re-frame her behaviour, she could see that the most helpful and protective thing she could do for her daughter would be to help her to gain a greater sense of independence.

The different understanding of what the family experiences had been certainly helped Miranda's mother to adjust her part in the relationship with her daughter. It did not 'cure' Miranda's dyslexia but it did mean that as her relationship with her mother changed she became more able to make use of the special needs help that was provided for her at school. As her confidence in her ability to learn started to grow she became much happier and secure in her friendships in class. The technique of re-framing is widely used in family therapy as a way of creating different explanations for family interactions than those that may have become unhelpfully fixed in the family's way of thinking. For Miranda's mother the crucial re-framing focused on different perspectives on what was protective; the facts of the situation were the same but the way they were thought about was different. The aim of re-framing is to offer alternative explanations for sequences and patterns of behaviour in such a way that new solutions can become more readily available. This latter feature distinguishes re-framing from interpretation because the alternative view is offered in an interactional context and explicitly points to new possibilities for how the relationship might develop.

In Miranda's case her teachers would be highly likely to have experienced similar frustrations to her mother in their failed attempts to help her be happier and more successful at school. Patterns often emerge between a teacher and child which closely resemble and reflect the dominant family relationships. Teachers can find themselves being pulled into relationships with a child that are not consistent with their usual ways of behaving. With Miranda it would be understandable if a teacher had attempted to get close to her to try to help her to talk about her difficulties. It would also be easy to appreciate if, in the face of failure to be 'successful' in helping Miranda, the teacher were to withdraw somewhat and adopt a less sympathetic position. Adopting a systemic perspective in this type of situation can be helpful for teachers as it offers a way for them of not feeling so personally responsible when relationships with a child don't always run smoothly. Should a teacher feel that they are being expected to adopt ways of behaving that are uncomfortable or beyond their normally successful repertoire it may be advisable to look in a different way at the overall situation.

As already mentioned, an anxiety regarding thinking systemically about children's behaviour and family relationships seems based on a reluctance to become involved with complexity. Having to deal with a 'difficult' child is hard enough, never mind choosing actively to engage with their family, especially when they are often also seen to be just as 'difficult'. This position represents a fundamental misunderstanding of the reason that so many people have adopted a systemic approach to their work with children and families. Thinking about behaviour in the context of significant relationships is useful as a way of introducing clarity and simplicity into situations that initially may appear unclear and impossible to resolve. Apparently complex behavioural patterns start to make sense and in so doing enable new solutions to be offered. Without a systemic understanding of why a child might be behaving as they do, the situation can frequently remain confused and solutions may be suggested that do not fit the child's actual predicament.

Aziz, 13 years old, presented teachers in his inner-city school with many difficulties through disruptive behaviour. He would walk out of lessons, often when there had been no apparent problem or significant challenge. He was never known to have completed homework and did not take equipment to his lessons. When talked to about his unacceptable behaviour or academic under-achievement he either would be very apologetic and compliant, or would become extremely abusive and storm out of the school. His teachers were confident that his poor academic performance was not due to significant learning difficulties: he spoke English fluently with good comprehension. When he left school he was seen to go off with another boy who also 'bunked off' and created similar difficulties for the teachers.

Throughout the whole of his Year 7, the school took a range of actions to try to help Aziz, as follows:

- He was given a number of detentions which he did not attend.
- His tutor learned that Aziz had a brother aged 17 and a sister aged 10. They seemed to live with their mother but there was no mention of the father. The family had come to Britain six months previously, as refugees from the Middle East, and the notes said that the family had received help from a refugee support organisation. Aziz's tutor found him defensive but able to acknowledge the difficulties at school. He promised her that he would improve. Aziz told her that when he left school he often went to the city centre

where young people were generally thought to be at risk of exploitation and/or harm.

- The tutor, head of year and the SENCO decided to monitor the situation more closely and to contact Aziz's family if his behaviour did not improve. The steady flow of increasingly exasperated complaints from teachers continued.
- Aziz's mother was invited to come to school to discuss worries about his behaviour. She attended with her elder son who acted as interpreter. She was worried about Aziz because he went into the city, sometimes until 1 a.m. She said that her two sons often argued and would end up fighting. On several occasions Aziz had called the police to get them to make his brother stop, but they had taken no action other than speaking to the boys. Neighbours were becoming angry at the level of noise coming from the flat. The tutor and head of year noticed that whenever anything was said about Aziz's behaviour, he would argue with her in Arabic. Although the teachers could not understand exactly what was being said it was clear that he was not willing to accede to her parental authority. Aziz's elder brother confirmed that he was telling her that she was wrong to talk about anything he did and that she had to shut up. Teachers noted that his mother appeared to capitulate in the face of Aziz's tirade. The elder brother explained that his mother did not want to upset Aziz because it would only make him angry.
- Aziz's behaviour continued to deteriorate and after being involved in a serious fight he was excluded for three days. A pattern of such incidents followed by short-term exclusions then developed. Aziz's mother consistently attended appointments when asked, but the teachers became discouraged at her apparent inability or unwillingness to assert parental authority. Aziz was moved to a different group because of particular difficulties with some boys in his tutor group. This did not make any difference to the pattern of his behaviour. The deputy head became involved and Aziz was allocated a full-time learning support assistant to help him manage. A view was developing that if things didn't start to improve the school would be forced to consider permanent exclusion. Aziz increased the frequency of his walking out of lessons and his truanting from school. Teachers felt that social work intervention was necessary, and a referral was made. Aziz stole a large amount of money and a mobile phone from the teacher who had been expending the most energy in trying to arrange appropriate help for him. The school senior managers felt that

they had no alternative other than to seek Aziz's permanent exclusion from the school.

What more could the teachers have done? They had offered Aziz much support, they had liaised closely with his mother, they had used the system of reward and sanctions available in school but still nothing seemed to help. Once the request for support from Aziz's mother had been unsuccessful, communication with the family was formal with little expectation of anything useful. Teachers began to consider Aziz's mother ineffectual and took on more and more responsibility for finding solutions from within the school's resources. At the same time, staff felt that Aziz's problems were not to do with school but with his family.

The key point here is that once the normal school strategies were seen not to be working, an opportunity was missed to use resources differently (Plas 1986). Rather than spend time and energy on solutions that were almost inevitably bound to fail, it could have been more effective to understand why Aziz was behaving in this way. Rather than doing more and more of the same, it is often useful to look for different information that has greater potential to make a difference. The obvious starting point would be to try to understand how he had learned to form relationships. The most helpful source for this information is invariably the family.

Aziz's capacity to become a successful learner at school was being seriously impaired by his difficulty in forming stable relationships, with teachers and peers alike. So what had Aziz learned about relationships in his family? He remembered his father shouting at his mother, and her attempts to defend herself ending in capitulation in order to keep the peace. When he was five his father left: Aziz learned that he couldn't persuade him to stay. He felt angry with his mother for letting his father go but soon understood that he had to hide these feelings to avoid critical comments from his elder brother. Despite enjoying his special situation as the youngest son in his Muslim family, he did not have his father's guidance to help him manage the subtleties not only of a boy's privileges but also of the responsibilities associated with such a position. After his father left, his brother spent a lot of time with his grandparents and his younger sister became the main source of solace for his mother. He learned to get his mother's attention by doing something wrong which could not be ignored. When he was 10, one of his mother's cousins angered the political regime and the family were harassed by the secret police. He saw his mother questioned harshly and witnessed the secret police coming to arrest her. Aziz tried to defend her but was unable to stop them from dragging her away. She was imprisoned for four months and brutally tortured, all the time tormented by worry about what was happening to her children. The family was only able to leave when relatives paid a ransom to secure his mother's release.

After coming to Britain, no help had been put in place for Aziz that made sense to him. Within the family nobody really appreciated the extent of the traumas that Aziz had experienced. He had learned to shut off his emotions from a young age. It is easy to imagine the damaging effect on a young boy of being unable to protect his mother and save her from imprisonment and torture. It is also easy to underestimate the impact of this event on a boy who already had sensitivities associated with earlier family experiences. It is also possible to understand Aziz's mother's predicament about trying to set limits for her youngest son while she felt guilty about her failure to protect him.

What difference does having this enriched information make? It enables professionals to have a better appreciation of the situation, so that Aziz will not be so easily dismissed as just another delinquent adolescent. His mother can no longer be simply thought of as 'ineffectual', even though she will still need to be helped to adjust her parenting so that she can help prevent Aziz from growing up as a disaffected and disconnected bully, particularly towards women. As one of the other parents who was attending the Education Unit said to Aziz's mother, 'I'll still tell you not to give in to him and to not give him money whenever he demands it, but I won't say it in such a harsh way as I used to.' Perhaps most important, Aziz's behaviour should not be seen as a personal challenge to the teacher. He is not deliberately seeking to attack or reject his teachers, rather, he is trapped in a habitual style of relating that is part of an abusive pattern.

Conclusion? Developing a systemic approach

Is this a 'can of worms'? It may seem so at first, but nothing would be likely to help him survive in society, let alone school, without attempts to understand what Aziz had learned about key relationships.

The two case illustrations have come from both ends of the severity continuum. In each situation however, being curious enough to find out more about the children's relational blocks to learning was a vital part of helping them be more successful at school and at home. As stated earlier, it is not clear whose job it is do this work; it is certain however, that it is a job that is worthwhile and needs doing.

A systemic approach offers the chance for teachers and associated educational professionals to develop a distinctly different method of thinking about, and intervening with, troubled and troubling children at school. It can reduce the impact of stigma and blame as well as producing practical solutions in many difficult situations. It is economical as it does not rely on the development of a long term therapeutic relationship. It focuses on producing new solutions to old problems within a short time so that a child can resume concentration on their main educational task as quickly as possible. It is a method that is even-handed as everybody takes a share of the problem but also has the opportunity to be helped to do something different to change the situation.

It would be wonderful if the relationships between teachers and parents could change in a way so that the phrase 'liaising with parents' is banned from school brochures and policy statements. As used, this frequently reflects a relationship based on one-directional information giving. Parents are rarely encouraged to liaise with teachers. With this fundamental imbalance in the teacher–parent relationship there is little scope for developing a shared systemic exploration. Teachers intuitively understand the family systemic forces that affect the children they teach. If training in the basic principles of a systemic approach could be offered there would enormous potential for redressing the power balance with families so that a much clearer shared understanding of the child could evolve. A genuine curiosity about how a child learns and develops both socially and emotionally if explored by teachers and parents together would enrich the educational experience for everybody.

References

Bowlby, J. (1971) *Attachment and Loss. Vol.1, Attachment*, Harmondsworth: Penguin.
Chiron, C., Jambaque, I., Nabbout, R., Lounes, R., Syrota, A. and Dulac, O. (1997) 'The right brain hemisphere is dominant in human infants', *Brain*, 120(6): 1057–65.
Cooklin, A. (1982) 'Change in here-and-now systems vs. systems over time' in A. Bentovim, G. Gorell-Barnes and A. Cooklin (eds) *Family Therapy: Complementary Frameworks of Theory and Practice*, London: Academic Press.
Dawson, N. and McHugh, B. (1986a) 'Families as partners', *Pastoral Care in Education*, 4(2): 102–9.
Dawson, N. and McHugh, B. (1986b) 'Application of a family systems approach in an education unit', *Maladjustment and Therapeutic Education*, 4(2): 48–54.

Dawson, N. and McHugh, B. (1987) 'Talking to parents of children with emotional and behavioural difficulties', *British Journal of Special Education*, 14(3): 119–21.

Dawson, N. and McHugh, B. (1988) 'Claire doesn't talk: behavioural or learning difficulty', *Gnosis*, 12, 8–11.

Dawson, N. and McHugh, B. (1994) 'Parents and children: participants in change' in E. Dowling and E. Osborne (eds) *The Family and the School: a Joint Systems Approach to Problems with Children*, London: Routledge.

Dowling, E. and Taylor, D. (1989) 'The clinic goes to school: lessons learnt', *Maladjustment and Therapeutic Education*, 7(1): 24–31.

Minuchin, S. (1974) *Families and Family Therapy*, London: Tavistock [1991: Routledge].

Plas, J. M. (1986) *Systems Psychology in the Schools*, New York: Pergamon.

Schore, A. N. (1994) *Affect Regulation and the Origin of the Self*, Mahwah NJ: Lawrence Erlbaum.

Schore, A. N. (2000) *Affect Regulation and The Repair of the Self*, New York: Guilford Press.

9 Prospective institutional inequities, interculturalism and education in Britain

Jagdish Gundara

Identities and education

This chapter is an attempt to develop some major issues in intercultural education as they are manifested within the now devolved British context and the context of the enlarging European Union. Although reference will be made to current English educational policy and practice in relation to national diversity, the principal purpose is to examine some of the issues that underpin such policy and practice but which in themselves are seldom analysed. The consequences of this lack of analysis, in England at least, are profound. Much of the work in relation to education in and for a multicultural society in Britain contains internal contradictions, and, more important, is ineffective in both reducing the discriminatory and prejudiced behaviour of many white pupils, teachers and students and in improving the educational attainments of many groups of minority students. Schools cannot assume that young people have singular oppositional or binary ethnicised identities (Walzer 1982).

The first point to highlight is the confusion that often arises over the use of the terms Briton, Britain and British. The confusion is at its most disturbing when used by the English. To many English people, English/British, England/Britain are synonyms. Clarification of this, a task that the Scots, Welsh and other British minorities find non-problematic, is both a starting point for analysis and leads to a re-examination of concepts of the nation, nationality(ies), nationalism and the nation state. By implication, intercultural education in the devolved contexts of England, Scotland and Wales needs to build on historical features of commonalities, shared interests and layers of friendship. A failure to deal with this issue with delicacy and intelligence can lead to xenophobia, chauvinism and increased racism (Commission for Racial Equality 1988), particularly because multiple identities are a norm in most schools, institutions of the state and society. Singular identities whether at national or ethnic level are an exception rather than the rule.

Most, if not all, nation states are stratified poly-ethnic states using a variety of mechanisms to maintain their social and economic stratification, usually sustained by an accompanying rhetoric emphasising societal cohesion (Gundara and Jones 1992). Stratification operates through criteria additional to those of class/status and gender, because of the way in which the state is constructed, structurally and ideologically. It is not surprising that the modern nation state is based on a fallacious ideal-typical model of a small scale society. The modern unitary nation state disguises its predatory origins by attempting to demonstrate a hegemonic unity in terms of its citizens, allegiances and affiliations. It is more likely that socially diverse states would remain cohesive if they are democratic and have effective measures to bring about greater levels of equity and stability.

Unity which is based on codification of the dominant groups' social and economic arrangements and an unequal set of socio-economic arrangements can lose its legitimacy if other groups question such inequalities. It is often the case that the process of stratification asserts that access to membership of that nation requires:

- the capacity to operate within certain linguistic and economic parameters; and
- acceptance of notions of a dominant 'common' history, religion and other socio-cultural factors.

Groups and individuals who do not conform to this pattern get constructed as outsiders. The 'aliens' and the 'other' lack cohesive capacity by definition and are seen to be a divisive element within the nation. Dominant groups often see themselves as the legitimately constituted nation, and use the 'others' as a means of maintaining such an ideological fiction. This perspective helps to position many minority ethnic and racial groups as dependent and at the periphery of the nation, in cultural, political, economic as well as spatial terms. Devolution can also unleash a new dynamic. The English minorities in Scotland and Wales can be constructed as 'the other' and become targets of discrimination. In turn there can be negative consequences for ethnic and national minorities in England, within the education system.

The marginalisation process has a long history in the British context which has been well illustrated by the work of Hechter (1975). As his analysis suggests, the denial of a capacity to belong to the nation leads to marginalisation of the groups who are so positioned, some because they can be 'racially' defined (as is the case with black people in the British context), and others because they can be defined as 'different' (the case of the Irish). This analysis has clear implications both for British cities, where the great majority of Britain's black population live, and for the education that is provided. The educational prospects of these groups would be further threatened in devolved systems unless the education ministries in Cardiff, Edinburgh and London plan to legitimise the integrity of multiplicity and obviate increases in racism and institutional discrimination in education.

Successive British governments have, with the confused idea of 'Britishness' mentioned earlier, tied themselves up in knots of ever more complex immigration and nationality laws, with intent to preserve the nation from being 'swamped' by alien – that is, black – cultures (Joppke 1999). It is difficult to see how such an exclusive state can remain cohesive if the subordinated groups are defined out of the concept of the nation, and can only belong through a process of self-denial and rejection of their own identities. What is perhaps surprising, and is most certainly a cause of equally serious concern, is the marginalisation of certain groups within the British nation state who are not immigrant. In other words, many black British citizens remain as marginalised as their immigrant ancestors. However, this pattern of discrimination can also begin to include the poorer English, Irish, Scottish and Welsh nationalities in other parts of devolved Britain.

The consequent racist stratification in Britain, as in many other nation states, sustains and creates national divisions that result in advantaged and disadvantaged groups having unequal access to power and resources. And it is the reproduction of this through the education system that helps to ensure its inter-generational continuation. An example of this process can be seen in the history and contemporary position of the long established black community in Liverpool. Still regarded as in some way not British, primarily because they are black, they are economically and socially marginalised within a city that is itself in a similar position *vis-à-vis* the southeast-dominated British nation state. Their educational attainment continues to remain at a very low level, despite community efforts to make the education system more responsive to their educational needs (Department of Education and Science 1985). Other groups could become similarly excluded if a narrow nationalistic response to becoming more inclusive were followed.

Furthermore, the failure in both imagination and policy by government that has led to an increasing ethnic and racial socio-spatial differentiation in the cities of Britain, has serious implications for inner city school populations. For example, in Tower Hamlets, an inner city borough in London, where 46 per cent of the primary pupils speak a language other than English as their first language, there are twenty-nine schools (out of a total of ninety-five) where the majority of pupils have a home language other than English and at least two where none of the children have English as their home language. This is a trend which the open admissions policies introduced by the 1988 Education Act is likely to intensify, for the Act enables white parents to withhold their children, if they wish, from schools with a high percentage of black pupils. Similar to the argument that took place some decades ago in the USA, separate schools for black and white children are, in the vast majority of cases, as inherently unequal here as they were (are) there.

This issue has a long legacy on both sides of the Atlantic. In Britain recently the Stephen Lawrence Inquiry chaired by Sir William Macpherson recommended changes in schools, teacher education and the curriculum (Macpherson 1999). It is now slowly being accepted that institutional discrimination exists and that it needs to be dealt with across the whole system.

Intercultural aims and objectives

The intercultural education agenda in schools implicates their aims and objectives, staff development, their curriculum and pedagogy. In examining these areas it is necessary to make problematic the concept of the intercultural curriculum and the school knowledge that the use of this term often involves, since it may invalidate the many knowledges that students in British schools bring to the learning environment.

Whatever the national government says regarding anti-racism or the aims and objectives of intercultural education, most schools have considerable say in setting their own aims and objectives and there is room for planned intervention at the individual school level. Schools may assert that they wish to provide a climate for positive intercultural learning where all (students and staff) feel equally valued. However such aims and objectives have to be made more tangible if they are to have positive value. They have to be converted into clear school policies that cover all aspects of school life and which are 'owned' by all who work there.

Notwithstanding the relative autonomy of schools in relation to national guidelines, a policy based in a school and created solely from within the school is seldom likely to lead to a full sense of ownership.

This is because teachers and students are members of communities, minority and majority, and any school policy has to have some degree of moral and educational congruence with the communities which they are from and which, in the case of the teachers, they serve. An intercultural policy which does not achieve this legitimation may well fail, as the Burnage Report indicated (Macdonald *et al*. 1990). In that instance, an inner city comprehensive secondary school which claimed to have an excellent anti-racist policy, in fact had a policy which brought about a collapse in good intercultural relations within the school after a racial murder. One reason for this was the fact that local minority or majority communities had little to do with the drawing up of the school's anti-racist policy. This is not just an issue of legitimation, it is also that a vital source of expertise or the source of racism was ignored.

However, the need to seek community expertise and legitimation may raise as many issues as it may solve. For example, if the school serves a community which has powerful racist elements within it, how may it reasonably expect approval for an anti-racist or an intercultural policy from that particular group? For instance if the community is fundamentalist, how are issues of an inter-faith nature to be dealt with? And if schools are competing for pupils in a declining demographic environment, as is often the case in inner city areas, management in schools may find such negative responses particularly difficult to handle if they feel the school roll is declining as a result of the introduction of an intercultural education policy. However, this argument could equally work the other way, since a positive commitment to intercultural education, evolved in conjunction with the school's communities, may very likely improve the reputation of a school. The urban experience of many schools would certainly support this latter perspective. The involvement and continuing education of adults in the community may help to deal with negative aspects of patriarchy, fundamentalism and racism.

The diversity that many schools face is not dealt with easily. How any school can resolve the issues raised by the range of cultures present both within the society at large and within the catchment area of the school itself is a matter of debate. It includes the issue of the relationship between education and religious beliefs and practices. Schools face a dilemma when setting out their aims and objectives because of issues posed in such a complex environment. Two examples illustrate the point. On the one hand, if a group or a community (not the state) want to deny girls or women access to education or employment, then the state has a right to intervene because such a particularistic practice would deny girls or women their right. On the other hand, the cultural practice of a Sikh wearing a turban or Muslim girls wearing a head-dress are legitimate acts because they do not impair acquisition of education or skills or capacity.

In general terms, church and state are divided for good reasons. In Britain the connection between the Crown and the Anglican Church still exists, although the society is largely considered secular (Gundara 1993). However, secularism is sometimes viewed as a modern paganism and conflated with humanism. Humanism is a philosophical system in which humanity not divinity is central. Secularism, however, can be seen largely as a legal system which provides the necessary framework to nurture equality for all citizens at the public level and which safeguards the sacred at the private level. Such a secular collectivity is not necessarily theistic, atheistic or agnostic. It therefore optimally provides a 'nest' for all groups and has a role to protect their citizenship rights. 'Positive secularism' or 'the nest' in this sense goes beyond merely the religious toleration of other groups (Verma 1986). It entails an understanding by all citizens and students of the shared values that are held in complex societies by the diverse groups that make up that society. This particularly entails the challenge of ensuring that children do not exclude certain values and groups in their individual mental maps. Thus, ideally, the school can potentially seek to become such a 'nest' for all children. The school therefore has the integrity of an institution which recognises the legitimacy of the multiple identities within it and its community. The school has a role to promote the safety and security of the school and its community. Not all parties to the formulation and implementation of educational policies would agree to this formulation.

The previous Conservative government's White Paper, for example, emphasised spiritual and moral development and stated 'Proper regard should continue to be paid to the nation's Christian heritage and traditions in the context of both religious education and collective worship in schools' (Department for Education 1991: 9). It is not sufficient to treat education in a multifaith society in this manner. The opportunity given to other faiths for worship remains withdrawal, suggesting that only Christianity has a recognised status. As a result, in many parents' and children's minds, other faiths remain second class and exotic. This detracts from understanding of other faiths and is divisive. Such divisiveness may in turn lead to conflict, with minority faiths being equated with fundamentalism, as has increasingly happened in relation to Islam in Britain. A consequence of this is that British Asians get constructed as 'Muslim fundamentalists' and issues of religious and racial equality are thrown to the winds.

This raises questions at two levels. First, how can schools help ensure that Muslims and others of different faith communities will receive equal educational treatment? More broadly, how can schools tackle the wider issue that the religious debates evoke, namely the appropriation by the white English of feelings, ways of seeing and understanding of those British citizens who are not white English, who are classified as the 'other' and whose voices are often ignored, both by the schools and the wider society.

Schools whose aims fail to address these intercultural needs of both groups of children, majority and minority, may, in their consequent practice, help to sustain both racism and fundamentalism in the school and the wider society. Indeed, part of the explanation for the increase in fundamentalism in modern *de facto* secular societies may be because such states have failed to provide a safe and secure framework for their various faith communities. As a consequence, religious and values education may merit a renewed sensitivity in schools. At the same time, the negotiation of values through public education should be limited to the values of the secular state within the public domain. The school in a plural society should by definition not interfere in the private and in the autonomous domain of the individual, because the essence of pluralism is the recognition of and respect for diverse lifestyles and belief systems in the private domain of families, groups and individuals. However, the school as a social institution does have the right to foster and nurture the common good of all members of the school and the society of which it is a part. It may therefore not wish to ignore religious *knowledge* and values as they relate to the values of a diverse secular society, just as ethical, spiritual and philosophical knowledge is part of the public domain and can be taught, partly to achieve the aim of religious tolerance which is a prerequisite for the maintenance of democracy (Gundara 1993). In contrast, religious *instruction* belongs to the private domain.

The example of religion demonstrates the difficulties that schools have to face if they are to articulate aims, objectives and policies that make educational sense and which meet the needs of all their pupils, whether from minority or majority backgrounds. Similar debates need to be undertaken by schools in relation to their integrity as an institution, so that they can connect with such issues as multilingualism and the school's position in relation to xenophobia, racism and discrimination. Clearly it is no easy task, particularly at a time of increased racism.

The intercultural curriculum

In multicultural communities, schools are important institutions because they can forge connectivity between different communities. They can also obviate the loss of cultural memory within such communities and within the school itself. An intercultural curriculum would enable schools not only to reduce ethnocentricity but to enhance aspects of plurality and greater levels of equity.

If curriculum entitlement is to an ethno-centric curriculum, it is no entitlement. A narrowly defined curriculum can reflect an ideological construction of the 'other's' past, and a heavily biased and one-sided view of the state, its history, languages, music, art, geography and so on. The transmission of such a curriculum assumes that there is a monocultural present as well as a monocultural past and future. Such an assumption is a fallacy and endangers the polity. If the mainstream curriculum is not intercultural it cannot in substantive terms meet the complex needs of all children within schools.

Even within the constraints that are placed upon schools in relation to curriculum, an emphasis that avoids narrow ethnocentrism and Anglocentrism is possible. To achieve this, schools need to regularly re-examine their curriculum offering, particularly as we learn more about the nature of British history and thought. For example, the pioneering work of Bernal (1990) points out that Greece, the embodiment of the intellectual and cultural childhood of Europe, acquired vast learning by borrowings from the Egyptian and Phoenician civilisations (Gundara 1990). The recognition of culture as a socially plural construction is essential, and is not dissimilar to Bakhtin's (1981) conception of language as a socially plural construct in which our own speech is never entirely exclusively our own, but always heteroglossic and polyvocal. Hence, children bring diverse repertoires and learnt experiences to the school. Schools need to keep this pluralistic perspective to the fore in their curriculum offering, and acknowledge the role of culture and language at the border line between oneself and 'the other'.

However, the different languages and cultures present within our schools often do not have equal value in the curriculum, and the subordinated communities from which these emanate seldom have the educational or political power to assert their entitlements, especially if national curricular guidelines are hostile to such ideas. In such circumstances, it may seem very difficult for schools to make a positive impact. However, links with the minority communities will help schools and teachers deal with the complex value dilemmas. Moreover, teachers and schools have made considerable progress in this area.

Implementing intercultural curricula has been a productive and lively area for individual teachers, groups of teachers and schools in the past. When reflecting on the bases of the knowledge which is transacted in the school curriculum, it is important to see that in Britain and Europe the historical, linguistic and knowledge systems of 'other' cultures and civilisations are often defined out, and they are seen to be either un- or semi-civilised. This has a direct consequence in excluding the linguistic and knowledge systems of some of the groups who live in Britain. A prerequisite of any curriculum development is to include such important contributions, because failure to do so would entail the teaching of an Anglocentric curriculum.

The production and teaching of knowledge should best serve the needs of the whole community. One of the first things that those who are involved in curriculum development need to learn is to 'unlearn' what Williams (1959) describes as 'the inherently dominative mode'. In England, the literatures are not seen as a broadly based subject with a canon which cuts across cultural boundaries, but as English literature. In studying this subject a student ultimately comes close to being 'English', but does not necessarily understand about intercultural literatures.

Finally, it is important to note that the hidden curriculum of a school may be more subject to its own control. Cohen (1991) demonstrated that the learning process in the playground was where the more complex set of values and identities of the locality permeate the school. Within diverse inner city schools, for example, there are large numbers of disenfranchised white communities. A particular problem is how young white male members from these communities construct 'imagined identities' which rely on notions of inherently singular understanding of such complex localities. In other words, how does the neighbourhood and the playground enter the classroom in children's imaginations and what types of knowledge, skills and understandings do teachers and schools need to tackle these? Educational initiatives which ignore these complexities do so at great risk to the communities in which such initiatives are implemented.

One obvious and important conclusion emerges from this, namely that it is essential that the schools are seen as a safe and secure environment for all children from a diversity of communities. In many cases, greater awareness of these issues by the school can be the first step in understanding how such a hidden curriculum can be addressed within the formal curriculum and the more general arrangement of the school.

Pedagogy

At the centre of improving the quality of education is the interaction between teacher and taught. Gipps (1992) reviewed leading British classroom research studies, and identified key pedagogic issues for enhancing the quality of children's learning in primary schools. They may also have relevance for other levels of the system. A variety of teaching styles need to be considered, to respond to the diversity of learning styles in classrooms. Such a shift of emphasis can support teachers having higher expectations of students by reducing negative stereotypes of some styles of learners. Classrooms of integrity would also be structured to encourage students expressing themselves to their peers. Cooperative learning can enhance the different statuses of children and validate difference and enhance intercultural understandings (Gundara 1992). Such classroom organisation would encourage students to be independent and self-disciplined rather than merely respond to teachers. In such classroom conditions both the students and the teachers would ensure that the work they are given is appropriate to their progress and levels of attainment.

Such research findings echo the views of many teacher practitioners. But knowing is not the same as doing, so we need to consider issues of staff development. Through small scale manageable experiments, teachers and schools have a real possibility of improving the quality and attainment levels of all children, especially those, such as many minority students, who currently under-perform within the system.

Effective pedagogy can also address the issue of many children's unformed and less-than-rational explanations for poor social conditions, diversity and inequality. Children's understandings may be influenced by xenophobic, chauvinistic and fundamentalist views which might be nurtured through peer group cultures, families, politicians and the media. In a diverse classroom, a simplistic engaging with such views can meet with a refusal to accept more rational explanations for issues like inequality, and the existence of refugees or immigrants. Well-structured cooperative learning strategies can provide ways of working in this controversial field that may well work better than a self-righteous and morally reproving stance.

Teachers and staff development

Initial teacher education requires rigorous intercultural courses for all teachers before they enter teaching. Continuing professional development is essential for teachers to maintain their knowledge and skill bases throughout their career. The Teacher Training Agency has been remiss in dealing with this issue, which concerns the professional skills, knowledge and intercultural understanding of all teachers.

The ever-changing peer group cultures, the changes in social class and nationality issues in relation to the developed state we live in should not be beyond the competence of teachers. In practical terms, the teacher has to create safe learning environments within which children's rights as well as their languages and religions are acknowledged. Staff development therefore needs to ensure that teachers' professional skills are refined not only to enable them to negotiate the curriculum in the classroom, but to understand the links between what happens in the classroom, the playground and the community.

In diverse classrooms with different hierarchies and statuses of children, teachers require support and appropriate staffing to ensure that cooperative learning for an intercultural and a non-centric curriculum is incorporated, and that it is effective in raising achievements of all children. Cooperative learning may promote mutuality in the learning process and negotiation of the curriculum. At the same time it may promote a certain autonomy to enable children to feel responsible as learners and as citizens. Staff development should ensure that teachers and their classroom communities can deal with incidents of racism in the classroom and minimise its effects.

Teachers can only negotiate the curriculum with pupils effectively if they are themselves enabled to have an open and critical mind. Given the increasingly complex range of issues at all levels that teachers confront in schools, they need to increasingly become their own researchers. They also need to maintain a critical perspective to the curriculum, and to the written and visual materials used.

A systematic and well resourced programme of staff development would ensure teacher retention, minimise teacher burn out and enable schools to have the confidence that their staff have up-to-date skills and competences. Staff development should not to be restricted to teachers, but include the whole school staff who impact on the whole school ethos.

Conclusion

To educate children for the future, the school needs to promote inclusive value systems and down-play the negative and divisive values inherited from the past. In the same process the school may become a more meaningful learning community. If terror exists in schools, children cannot learn and attain. In time, such changes ought to bring improved equalities of outcomes for all children.

Intercultural education does not offer a panacea for the complex social and economic problems currently affecting our society. Nevertheless, the school has a crucial role to play in the education of all children. As a result, intercultural learning has an original contribution to make in the education that is provided in *all* schools about living in a multicultural future. The common sense understanding that these issues are only relevant to diverse inner city schools is a mistaken one because the rural or monocultural schools also require intercultural education.

In the same way, educational initiatives which lead to making diversities cohere are an advantage, particularly during a period when many diverse societies are fragmenting. A school whose total educational offering de-emphasises racism and narrow ethnicities or nationalism can initiate the process which can in turn nurture and assist the development of learning for all its students. Standards of attainment for those currently failing in the system can be positively addressed and the unhealthy racism and xenophobia which hinders the education of so many students can be purposefully assailed. In other words, as teachers have always known, there is much that can be done to make our schools more effective learning institutions.

Devolution at local levels and European unification at the supranational levels which are evolving democratically, provides teachers, students, schools and communities with a creative moment to develop an inclusive curricula and shared and common values. The potential for multicultural citizenship is a distinct possibility if educators and policy-makers can capture the dynamic potential for societal change.

References

Bakhtin, M. (1981) *The Dialogic Imagination: Four Essays by Bakhtin* (trans. C. Emerson and M. Holquist), Austin TX: University of Texas.

Bernal, M. (1990) *Black Athena: the Afro-Asian Roots of Classical Civilisation*, New Brunswick NJ: Rutgers University Press.

Cohen, P. (1991) *Monstrous Images, Perverse Reasons: Cultural Studies in Anti-Racist Education*, London: University of London Institute of Education International Centre for Intercultural Studies.

Commission for Racial Equality (1988) *Learning in Terror*, London: CRE.

Department for Education (1991) *Choice and Diversity: a New Framework for Schools*, London: HMSO.

Department of Education and Science (1985) *Education For All*, 'The Swann Report', London: HMSO.

Gipps, C. (1992) *What We Know About Effective Primary Teaching*, London: University of London Institute of Education.

Gundara, J. (1990) 'Societal diversities and the issue of "The Other"', *Oxford Review of Education*, 16(1): 97–109.

Gundara, J. (1992) 'An Agenda for Intercultural Cooperative Learning', paper given to International Conference on Cooperative Learning, IASCE/International Association for Inter-cultural Education.

Gundara, J. (1993) 'Values, National Curriculum and diversity in British society' in P. O'Hear and J. White (eds) *Assessing the National Curriculum*, London: Paul Chapman.

Gundara, J. and Jones, C. (1992) 'Nation states, diversity and interculturalism: issues for British education' in K. Moodley (ed.) *Beyond Multicultural Education: International Perspectives*, Calgary: Detseling.

Hechter, M. (1975) *Internal Colonialism: The Celtic Fringe in British National Development*, Berkeley CA: University of California Press.

Joppke, C. (1999) *Immigration and the Nation State*, Oxford: Oxford University Press.

Macdonald, I., Bhavnani, R., Khan, L. and John, G. (1990) *Murder in the Playground: the Report of the Macdonald Enquiry into Racism and Racial Violence in Manchester Schools*, London: Longsight Press.

Macpherson, W. (1999) *Report of an Inquiry – The Stephen Lawrence Inquiry*, London: Home Office.

Verma, S. (1986) *Towards a Theory of Positive Secularism*, Jaipur: Ramat Publications.

Walzer, M. (ed.)(1982) *The Politics of Ethnicity*, Cambridge MA: Belknap Press.

Williams, R. (1959) *Culture and Society 1780–1959*, London: Chatto & Windus.

10 Schools for communities

John MacBeath

I was quick to dismiss the concept of the twenty-four hour school when it was first suggested in an informal conference discussion of educational researchers. A hundred and one good reasons presented themselves in rapid succession – too far from the obvious, too much beyond my comfort zone. Yet the subject generated such heat among normally rational researchers that it became a challenge worth pursuing. The case *for* was irretrievably lost by its proponents when the analogy of the supermarket was introduced. Its inherent 'market' assumptions were an ideological step too far. Nor did the example of hospitals do anything to advance the argument. Schools are not supermarkets and they aren't casualty or emergency centres. They are places for learning and learning is underpinned by a set of conventional premises. It requires teachers. It is structured and sequential. Its content and methodology are age-related. It requires an optimum size of age cohort at every level. Education is for children and children sleep at night. As do their teachers. And since children have parents, schooling must take account of parents' working hours and holidays and be tailored to the rhythms of the commercial and industrial world. Or so it was claimed.

Discussions about education seem always to return to this basic set of premises. The schoolhouse is such a powerful icon and has survived a millennium virtually unchanged. Those who have passed through it have faithfully reproduced it generation after generation. Schooling as we know it is a classic example of the phenomenon of 'lock in' (Waldrop 1994), that is, a set of forces with such a powerful inertia that there is no entry point for change. One of the classic examples of 'lock in' cited by Waldrop is the 'qwerty' keyboard, designed in an age when the pressing of a typewriter button mechanically pushed up a metal lever (also called a 'key'), the most frequently used metal keys having to be kept as far apart as possible to avoid jamming. Not only has the keyboard survived into an electronic age but its quaint 'qwerty' design has as well because generations of secretaries and schoolchildren have been trained in its use.

Schools as we know them are similar self-sealing systems and radical attempts to change them have either been outside the mainstream, in the independent sector, or have enjoyed a brief beleaguered life before retreating to a more familiar and comfortable set of structures. The community schools of the 1970s and 1980s are deemed by conventional wisdom to have been a failure – a gloss on history which has suited politicians and policy-makers and their spin doctors.

It is ironic that the schools that ushered in the twenty-first century are in some respects closer to schools of the 1940s and 1950s than to those of the 1970s and 1980s. However much they may have embraced technologies unimaginable in the 1970s, they are less adventurous, less open-minded, ill-equipped pedagogically to embrace the brave new world. The more demand-led approaches of the 1970s are seen to be discredited and the prescription for schools is to tighten their boundaries, and their 'delivery systems'. The term delivery is an increasingly apt one for what teachers are being asked to do, although there is a curious contradiction in the language of the marketplace on the one hand, and an increasingly deterministic view of teaching and learning on the other.

There is also an interesting set of anomalies when it comes to education post-sixteen. This tends to be seen as the point when lifelong learning begins, when the full blown consumer model comes into its own and the adult learner, with learning credits to spend, can choose a variety of places and pathways to further learning. This rests on the assumption that despite lack of experience of critical choice, or practice in the exercise of initiative and risk-taking, the dependent classroom-learner will move to independent, self-driven learning in a single bound.

While a salient strength of British primary schools in the past few decades has been in allowing children opportunity to exercise responsibility and develop generic skills, the move to secondary schools has often brought with it a more constrained and limited range of experiences. The deeply ingrained view of secondary education, through the lens of 'academic subjects', is an input view. It is one in which 'subjects' dictate the rhythms and structures of school life. So target setting is reduced to measures of acquisition of inputs rather than skills, and left to one side are the 'spiritual, moral, cultural, mental and physical development' observed only in high rhetoric.

Structures of subject departments have inhibited the development of 'convergent modalities' (Siler 1997) or 'transversal competences' (European Commission 2000), that is skills and understandings which transcend individual disciplines and enable students to carry their learning from one context to another. While on the one hand we are coming to acknowledge these as crucial to thinking, creativity and problem-solving, on the other we seem to be encouraging a trend back to 'subjects', even in primary schools, so threatening to undermine the exciting thematic work which was characteristic of the brightest and best of primary practice in the 1960s and 1970s. Powerful influences, through the medium of newspapers and popular journals, have appealed to the lowest common denominator of expectations in order to advance their own political purposes. In 1998 the Chief Inspector of schools wrote: 'All this, as I say, is little more than common sense. There is nothing new under the sun when it comes to good classroom teaching' (Woodhead 1998: 31). This neatly encapsulates the dilemma. In response to such an educationally feeble but politically powerful statement the system is re-geared to 'train' teachers to deliver a curriculum more efficiently to classes of thirty plus pupils because methodology is 'obviously' where the problem lies and a powerful political ideology, endorsed in high places, asserts that good teaching is all we need to compensate for the world beyond the classroom. The Chief Inspector continued:

> I do not accept the argument that a child who has a free school lunch is a child who will necessarily find it difficult to read . . . If they are fortunate enough to have it [a good teacher], then, as test and inspection evidence shows, there is no reason why they cannot do as well as children from more privileged backgrounds.

These words have the comforting logic of common sense but conceal a magnificent myth which is both gross and pernicious. Schools *can* make a difference but they cannot make all the difference and after three decades of school effectiveness research world-wide we know beyond any reasonable doubt that it is what happens *outside* schools that is the most significant factor in determining school success and in influencing life chances. The 1970s claim that schools could only reduce inequality at the margins has not been substantially undermined by three decades of school effectiveness research.

'Lock in' and the continued inability of schools to make a significant difference for all may be explained by their 'vertical' and 'horizontal' dimensions. The horizontal relationship is in the connections between school and community and is tested by the permeability of the boundaries between home and classroom, school and street. The 'vertical' relationship is what ties schools into an upward progression, nursery to primary, primary to secondary, secondary to college and university.

Historically, for children from working-class families and communities, upward progression through the system created tensions with the horizontal networks, because as children progressed through the system it opened up a distance between them and their families and communities (Jackson and Marsden, 1966). While this analysis may not apply in such acute form in the year 2000 it is a cultural legacy slow to be undermined (Freedland 1999). Comprehensive schools, once seen as the guarantors of comprehensive education, have failed to equalise outcomes, or even access, in part because they have been obliged to exist alongside selective schools, assisted places, parental choice and league tables. In combination these have formed interlocking pieces, ensuring an upward progression for a minority but leaving in their wake a 'problem' to be solved within a parallel, more community-oriented system.

Education Action Zones in England and New Community Schools in Scotland are innovative attempts to break free from the structures and conventions that have failed disadvantaged children and young people. However, the constant additions – new initiatives, endless fresh starts, privately endowed 'academies' – do nothing to dislodge the assumption that the gold standard is the traditional grammar school in which real education takes place and which is simply a prelude to a university education.

In different senses of the word this may be seen as a system lacking in integrity. Integrity in terms of a commitment to education for all. Integrity in the sense of structures and supports designed to meet such a commitment. Integrity in the sense of ensuring that children, young people and adults experience a coherence and progression in their learning.

The society of the 2000s will never see a return to community schools as we once knew them and it would be disingenuous to contemplate such a possibility. But we can explore new ways of linking school education with more integrity to the education that takes place in the large proportion of time which children and young people spend out of school. Rather than discarding the twenty-four hour school out of hand we should explore its possibilities. It may prove an idea too far but as on any journey of discovery we may alight on something new and unexpected.

Challenging assumptions

The first assumption to be challenged by the twenty-four hour school is that education is for children. The 'front end' model of education is one which presupposes that children are taught all the things they need to know before being let loose on the world, but such an assumption is less and less relevant in a society in which learning is becoming a lifetime commitment, and where education takes place in a multiplicity of sites and in diverse sets of relationships.

> If children grow up considering knowledge to be something that is merely handed down by teachers, for reasons that are somewhat obscure to the student, they are far less likely to continue learning in adult life than if learning is seen as a voluntary voyage of discovery.
>
> (Bentley 1998: 17)

The age cohort model with automatic promotion year on year is questionable on a number of grounds, especially when we examine the power of educational relationships in other contexts such as the family, or in other social organisations such as churches, interest groups, hobby and leisure clubs or community centres.

Hannon's (1993) comparison of school and home as contexts for learning is instructive.

School learning	*Home learning*
• shaped by curriculum	• shaped by interest
• bounded by sanctions	• spontaneous
• timetabled	• flexible
• contrived problems	• natural problems
• restricted language	• everyday language
• limited conversations	• extended conversations
• special resources – limited access	• 'natural' resources – unlimited access
• recognition of achievement in approved areas	• recognition of achievement in many areas
• horizontal age group	• vertical age group
• distant relationship with adults	• close relationship with adults
• pupil role	• multiple roles
• accounts for little variation in academic achievement	• accounts for much variation in academic achievement

Of special significance in the above lists are vertical age groups and multiple roles. The character of learning when young children interact with older children and adults is essentially different from that in the horizontal age cohort. Researchers (for example, Willms 1985; Sammons *et al.* 1996) have identified a 'compositional effect' which more often than not drags down individual attainment because the reference point for expectations and aspirations is the immediate peer group, more often than not suspicious of those who try too hard (Harris 1998). Nor does the age-related structure of schools allow much scope for multiple roles. The current structure of schools 'teaches' above all the pupil role. Teachers teach and pupils learn and it rarely happens the other way around. The following example from a teacher illustrates what can happen in a different relationship, generally outside school where the constraints of curriculum and role are no longer relevant.

> Three lads came to see me wanting to start a guitar club. They wanted space to do it and support. They wanted to advertise it and run it themselves and a teacher to supervise. It was a spur of the moment thing but I suppose I intuitively recognised the opportunity it offered me. I volunteered to be the supervising teacher because I play the guitar myself. Badly I have to say. As the supervising teacher I had nothing to do except keep an eye on things, watch and listen. I became a regular member. They were a million miles ahead of me in guitar technique. They recognised that pretty quickly too and helped me along from where I was, not from their pinnacle of expertise. Gently but challengingly too. They were excellent teachers. They taught me so much. I think I learned a bit too about organisation and teamwork and something about pedagogy as well.
>
> (MacBeath and Myers 1999)

This example tells us something important about learning. Its character here is closer to tutoring or coaching than to teaching. In this relationship there is a greater fluidity and interchangeability of teacher and learner roles. It is a microcosm of what a school might be like if it could exceed its conventional parameters and open up itself to the possibilities of collaborative learning.

In a Chicago High School a number of students offered me their business cards – suppliers of electronic hardware, technical services, builders and repairers of computers, consultants on ICT. One, Curtis L. Taylor, Chief Executive of Dinatron, aged 16, spent a fair proportion of his time, during and after school, teaching his teachers. In elementary school he had offered to run a professional development day for his teachers. He had drawn up a development plan and costed staff in-service. The school had, in the event, not taken him up on the offer, perhaps because it was at that time a role challenge too far.

In Information and Communication Technology many pupils are ahead of their teachers and can teach them a lot given the opportunity. In personal and social education schools are increasingly recognising the futility of teachers 'teaching' about sex, relationships and drugs when young people themselves often have a much better insight into curricular content and methodology in these areas.

A major British multinational company uses a points weighting in recruiting new staff, with top credits going to recruits who have been an organiser or president of a school club, or an editor of a school, university or community newspaper, or who have had involvement or leadership in a local political party. Points (on a five point scale) are also awarded to positions such as stage manager or producer, organiser of a charity drive, dance or other large function, or a responsible role in the family business.

How do children and young people acquire the skills and the confidence to be leaders, organisers, key players, joiners, participants in their schools? Are these the same skills and attitudes which help them to cope effectively with the curriculum and to expect success? The answer is that there is a very considerable overlap between the joiners and leaders and the academically successful because both are underpinned by a confidence and sense of self, developed at home, in school and in the interface between the two.

Coleman (1998) describes the critical teacher–pupil–parent relationship as 'the power of three'. We can represent this diagrammatically as a triangle, with pupil, teacher and parent at the apexes and each of the sides marked by a plus or minus to denote the positive or negative nature of the relationship. Substitute a minus on any one of the three sides and educational energy and learning potential are diminished. Substitute two or three minuses for the pluses and the power of the educational relationship disappears entirely except for the most resilient and self-driven of individuals. As we have learned from Feuerstein *et al.* (1980), the difference between success and failure is less explained by what happens in schools and classrooms than by what happens beyond the school gates. Nor, as Feuerstein demonstrates, is the determining factor poverty *per se*. The key issue is how learning is mediated by parents, other adults or siblings. They can help to structure meaning for children and give the quality of support to their offspring which will shepherd them through the challenges of childhood, secure in the knowledge that there is a supporting hand behind them. This, as teachers are not slow to recognise, is a priceless asset. It provides a foundation on which to build in continuing concert with a concerned parent or parents.

Community schools revisited

If then the supermarket and hospital are too far away as analogues for the twenty-four hour school, what about libraries, resource centres, Cybernet cafés, community centres, social clubs, health, sports or fitness centres? Are these attractive venues for people to visit in their own time? What makes them attractive and what kind of places do people want to go of their own volition? Where can people learn to play the guitar if they want to? learn to paint or draw? learn to read or write or to improve those skills whatever their personal, social or professional purpose?

As we move increasingly into the twenty-four hour economy those needs are less and less subservient to the nine hour 'working day'. Work round the clock is now a reality for people in the fields of health, media, entertainment, transport, security, service and retail industries. People work, learn and sleep at different times, increasingly because we are in a world market which never closes. The global village doesn't go to bed and if you want to communicate directly with someone in another hemisphere you will probably not be able to do that within the traditional compass of the office, factory or school day.

If we think of schools as a real community resource for all ages, serving different educational and social purposes, the twenty-four hour school looks less and less far-fetched. In the twenty-four hour school the variety lies not simply in the range of opportunities for learning but in the different age and interest groups who may have access to resources of the school – and to one another. There can be individual access to computers, gymnasia, games halls, language listening posts, art and science resources. There can also be access to corporate events which bring together the resources of people of all ages – meetings, workshops, mini-conferences, planning groups, rehearsals, exhibitions, drama, artists and musicians in residence. And there can be informal and planned opportunities for individual and group work in academic and vocational studies.

While there is still room for a traditional school day within this structure it will, with time, become more and more of an anachronism. The experience of a more fluid set of activities and relationships will inevitably blur the boundaries between 'educational', 'social' and 'vocational' as people come to recognise that health, diet, exercise, organising and running projects, leading groups, sports, games and social intercourse can be as educative and life-enhancing as what is taught through the traditional curriculum. This does not in any way deny the possibility of 'direct teaching', the new mantra of policy-makers and chief inspectors. Much of the character of voluntary work, training and self-help groups includes direct teaching, but as appropriate to context, purpose, needs and learning styles.

The logistic issues around the notion of twenty-four hour schools recede in significance when we study the big picture, when we contemplate the sea change in thinking that twenty-four hour access to learning suggests. It is, perhaps, not such a remote possibility after all. Connecting bridges are already being built between this present and that future. A good example of this is study support.

'Study support' is the somewhat unfortunate name given to out-of-hours learning that has become such an integral part of Government policy in the last few years. The name, coined in the early days of homework clubs and supported self-study, came to have a broader umbrella meaning as out-of-hours centres expanded their repertoire and raised their expectations. A definition of study support given by the DfEE (1998) is:

> to raise achievement by motivating young people to become more effective learners through activities which enrich the curriculum and improve core skills. These activities take place on a voluntary basis out-of-school hours.
>
> (p. 3)

'Out-of-school hours', a defining characteristic of study support, covers a wide range of possibilities – twilight sessions, evenings, Saturdays, weekends, residential courses, Easter and summer schools, ongoing mentoring or coaching. Some of the earliest forms of out-of-hours provision were centres where young people could go to do their homework, nothing more elaborate or pretentious than a warm welcoming place to go after school. However, as homework clubs began to test their effectiveness and challenge their boundaries they began to mature into study support centres, widening their compass, focusing less on homework and more on learning. They recognised that homework could simply perpetuate bad habits and reinforce a mechanistic view of learning. They 're-cognised' (apprehended anew) that literacy and numeracy are not simply a product of intensive concentration on technical skills and that success in any area of the curriculum is intimately related to self-confidence, motivation, attitudes to learning and achievement in other spheres.

So out-of-hours learning centres began to include community initiatives, newspaper projects, film making and video editing, enterprise activities, thinking skills workshops, assertiveness training and other programmes focused on personal and social competencies. This breadth of purpose is reflected in the way that simple distinctions between 'work' and 'play', 'academic and 'non-academic' pursuits become blurred, and a wider, more inclusive view of learning is created. A wider view of relations and contexts also emerges, with young people working individually, co-operating in pairs or groups, in outdoor settings, engaged in problem-solving or team-building exercises, developing interests in sports or hobbies. 'Study support' may indeed be an inappropriate label to apply to such a diverse range of activities but until a new terminology emerges it will continue to signify that range of voluntary activities which takes place out of hours and which shares a set of common goals:

• to provide opportunities for success and achievement;
• to build self-confidence and self-esteem;
• to encourage a stronger engagement with school;
• to celebrate the intrinsic value of enjoyable and stimulating leisure activities; and
• to motivate and re-engage young people with learning.

The success of study support has confounded the expectations of just about everyone. What was it that brought young people back in the evening, on Saturday mornings, or for their Easter or summer holidays? What made teachers stay on or return to schools in the evening after a tiring and stressful day? What made parents want to lend a hand or support the work of centres in other ways? What brought in volunteers from the community and local business? Why did university students sign on to waiting lists to become involved? These questions need to be answered differently for different groups but there were common motives and common rewards too, such as enjoying a purposeful climate with the attendant rewards of achievement beyond expectation.

A striking feature of study support centres is their growth from the bottom up. They have developed organically, over time, through networks and self-evaluation. They have responded to demands. They have been learner-centred in character, marked by informality, spontaneity and flexibility, and above all they have been voluntary. The growth of study support nationally from small beginnings in the early 1990s to a major national 'movement' endorsed and financed by government agencies, illustrates the power of bottom up/top down, the paradigm for change now most widely recognised as the most effective (Fullan 1993).

Study support centres independently invented themselves in a variety of guises in many different communities. For example, in St Gemma's School in the Ardoyne district of Belfast the school opened four evenings a week until 10 o'clock at night, admitting anybody who wanted to come in and use the resources of classrooms, the library, teachers and others (adults or young people). On a good night as many as 150 children and adults aged from 7 to 70 passed through the centre. It started in order to meet a perceived need to offer opportunities for learning previously denied by a locked, shuttered and darkened building. Open into the night hours, St Gemma's quite literally shines through the darkness of the Ardoyne streets.

St Gemma's provided a place where young people could do their homework in peace away from the distractions of younger siblings and attractions of wallpaper television. But if that was the initial impulse for young people to become involved, its benefits began to assume a wider compass. Some young people discovered that it was not simply about getting homework done, or swotting joylessly for exams but about the fun of learning, sharing with others, discovering new ways of thinking, taking charge of your own goals. It was not just about meeting other people's demands and deadlines but about learning for yourself. Older students discovered the payback there was from helping younger pupils. Adults and students found they could work together across the boundaries of age, and 'ability' was no longer a relevant construct.

Ten years on St Gemma's is still there and the same inspirational people who have consistently supported it over a decade, and others too, are driving it forward. But its development has been sustained, at least in part, because it has been networked with other centres in Scotland, England and Wales and through workshops and exchange visits. Through reflective self-evaluation it has gained in confidence in what it was already doing well and with the added value of discovering how to do things better.

Miller (1995) argues that research remains to be done on the effects of out-of-school learning. He argues that just as investment in early childhood education is a worthy social policy goal, so concurrently we need the creation of opportunities for children and young people who have missed out and who continue to miss out either through lack of parental support or because the system has failed them.

The simplistic, and counter-productive, solution is the extended school day, but this is unlikely to help those already failed by the school because it simply offers more of the same, more of what has already produced disinterest and disaffection. On the other hand, a shorter school day with more opportunity for learning support, mentoring, coaching and community projects may prove to be the more effective route into young people's interests and affections. Gardner (1983) describes the successful student:

> he/she knows how to use opportunities for learning which are distributed throughout his or her environment. This includes not only books and libraries, media and electronic information, but the learning resources of people – teachers, friends, family, mentors and employers.
>
> (p. 35)

As well as the open access to resources for learning, much of what brings young people and adults into study support is the people resources, and the sociability of the environment. It is this factor indeed that keeps young people going to school even when they describe their subjects of study boring. In an ongoing study (Myers and MacBeath 1999), which includes evaluation of student attitudes to study support as well as mainstream teaching, only half of the 10,000 students said they found lessons interesting and one in five admitted to 'counting the minutes until the lesson ends', while over 96 per cent preferred lessons where they could work with other students. The disparities we find between the relatively high percentage who say they like school and the relatively low percentage who find lessons interesting is explained by the social pull of the school. When lessons exploit that social drive their interest and enjoyment level rises commensurately.

The greatest attractions of study support in England, Scotland and Northern Ireland are its voluntary nature, the informal context and easy-going relationships between students and teachers and the student-led agenda (MacBeath 1991, 1993). For disenfranchised young people, in some cases regular truants during the school day, out-of-hours provision offered a way back in that was congenial and collegial. Its informal character was not antithetical to high expectations and making demands on the learner. If success is intrinsically satisfying, as we now know with some certainty from neuroscience (Ornstein 1993), evolutionary biology (Pinker 1999) and psychology (Csikszentmihalyi

1990) then we need more places for success of the kind that study support offers.

As Gardner argues, successful students are independent learners. They know how to motivate themselves, how to plan, how to organise and how to use techniques of accelerated learning. But they are also inter-dependent learners, sharing and collaborating with one another. This presents a serious challenge to schools because many of them are not very good at supporting the development of independent and inter-dependent thought and action. As we discover more about learning we recognise its intensely social nature. It is in relationships between people that knowledge is created and tested. As a leading physicist puts it:

> Thought is largely a collective phenomenon . . . As with electrons we must look on thought as a systemic phenomenon arising from how we interact and discourse with one another.
>
> (Bohm 1996: 199)

So it is not simply a matter of a congenial social context, but a deeper form of learning that takes place when people explore ideas with one another. Hargreaves (1997) says:

> Social intelligence – the ability and sensitivity to understand and predict other people's mind and intentions, and behave skilfully in social relationships – has always been highly esteemed by employers. It is now seen by some evolutionary biologists and social scientists as the root of *all* intellectual development.

However, the benefits of study support and related initiatives are not simply for one generation of children who pass through. The success of study support should be measured by what it contributes to the resilience, imagination and innovative capacity of the system as a whole, including professional capacity-building for teachers. Freed from the pressure of the classroom, teachers report that they were able to stand back, to watch young people at work, and to reflect on how effectively they were learning (MacBeath 1991). Teachers spoke about study support as a laboratory, or an incubator, as a place where you try something out, plant the seeds of an idea, and watch it develop. As a testing ground for new approaches to learning and teaching, study support was seen as having an immense potential. It was an important source of continuing professional development. Teachers, by their own admission, were often not confident in helping young people to think for themselves or explore ideas, to investigate their own learning styles and comfort zones. The pressures to stay in control and 'cover' the syllabus left little time to engage in debate and exploit the spontaneous moments of insight and creative diversions.

There are far-reaching implications in this for policy and practice. Schools cannot provide the whole of education, and education is not synonymous with school. But schools can be recast in a new mould. In a newer mould they can broaden their curriculum, open themselves to a wider clientele, build alliances on the horizontal axis – with parents and community, with other agencies, with local community. Our single-minded focus on the nine-to-three school, our research and policy investment in improving it within its current parameters, has inhibited a wider understanding of learning and undermined a more coherent systemic approach to lifelong learning. Study support is just one way in which we can move beyond the logistics of school organisation and extend the boundaries of our thinking. The school which opens at seven thirty for breakfast clubs and access to libraries, and remains open until ten in the evening, is already seeing provision and opportunity in a different relationship. The inclusion of adults in a variety of roles is already exemplifying ways in which schools can become more responsive learning centres in their communities.

In closing

In 1992 the OECD predicted the erosion of the school as a geographical entity. They envisaged increased contact between teachers and learners in different institutions and settings and a move away from class-based teaching to individual learning. The Education 2000 group foresaw the New Millennium incorporating the following features:

- greater recognition of the contribution of young people to learning and teaching themselves and one another;
- facilities located in different community sites;
- flexibility of age groupings, shared and group learning as well as independent study;
- developing profiles and portfolios of competences instead of traditional examinations;
- learning provided at a variety of levels with easier exit and entry points;
- a teaching force with a better mix of people;
- contributions from and partnership with local employers; and

- a 'curriculum' including education in social and political processes, health, basic legal education, learning skills, personal and vocational counselling, education for parenthood/citizenship, survival skills, life skills.

Perhaps the twenty-four hour school is not such a daft idea after all. It will, however, require some millenarian thinking about logistics and roles, how to pay for services, new forms of accountability and partnership, new ways of empowering families and children. It will require the courage to ignore the siren voices, some of them emanating from the wings, some from centre stage. It will require integrity to do what is right, not simply in terms of what is good for politicians within their short political lifetime but what will be a sustainable infrastructure for all our future.

References

Bentley, T. (1998) *Learning Beyond the Classroom: Education for a Changing World*, London: Routledge.

Bohm, D. (1996) *Wholeness and the Implicate Order* (Reissue edition), London: Routledge.

Coleman, P. (1998) *Parent, Student and Teacher Collaboration: the Power of Three*, London: Paul Chapman.

Csikszentmihalyi, M. (1990) *Flow: the Psychology of Optimal Experience*, New York: Harper & Row.

DfEE (1998) *Extending Opportunities: A National Framework for Study Support*, London, Department for Education and Employment.

European Commission (2000) 'European Report on Quality of Education', Paper presented to European Ministers, Budapest, June.

Feuerstein, R., Rand, Y., Hoffman, M. A. and Miller, R. (1980) *Instrumental Enrichment: an Intervention Programme for Cognitive Modifiability*, Baltimore: University Park Press.

Freedland, J. (1999) *Bring Home the Revolution: the Case for a British Republic*, London: Fourth Estate.

Fullan, M. (1993) *Change Forces: Probing the Depths of Educational Reform*, London: Falmer Press.

Gardner, H. (1983) *Frames of Mind: the Theory of Multiple Intelligences*, New York: Basic Books.

Hannon, P. (1993) 'Conditions of learning at home and in school' in R. Merttens, D. Mayers, A. Brown and J. Vass (eds) *Ruling the Margins: Problematising Parental Involvement*, London: IMPACT Project.

Hargreaves, D. H. (1997) 'Equipped for Life', paper at ESRC seminar Revitalising Policy through Research, 25 June.

Harris, J. R. (1998) *The Nurture Assumption*, London: Bloomsbury.

Jackson, B. and Marsden, D. (1966) *Education and the Working Class*, Harmondsworth: Penguin.

MacBeath, J. (1991) *Learning for Yourself: Supported Study in Strathclyde Schools*, Glasgow: Strathclyde Regional Council/Jordanhill College.

MacBeath, J. (1993) *A Place for Success*, London: Prince's Trust.

MacBeath, J. and Myers, K. (1999) *Effective School Leaders*, London: Prentice-Hall.

Miller, B. M. (1995) *Out-of-school Time. Effects on Learning in the Primary Grades*, Action Research Paper 4, School-Age Child Care Project, Wellesely MA: Wellesley College Center for Research on Women.

Myers, K. and MacBeath, J. (1999) 'Evaluating Out-of-hours Learning', Paper presented at International Congress on School Effectiveness and School Improvement, San Antonio, January.

Ornstein, R. (1993) *The Roots of the Self*, San Francisco, Harper Row.

Pinker, S. (1999) *How the Mind Works*, London: Penguin.

Sammons, P., Mortimore, P. and Thomas, S. (1996) 'Do schools perform consistently across outcomes and areas?' in J. Gray, D. Reynolds, C. Fitz-Gibbon and D. Jesson (eds) *Merging Traditions: The Future of Research on School Effectiveness and School Improvement*, London: Cassell.

Siler, T. (1997) *Breaking the Mind Barrier: the Artscience of Neurocosmology*, New York: Touchstone Press.

Waldrop, M. M. (1994) *Complexity: the Emerging Science at the Edge of Order and Chaos*, London: Penguin.

Willms, J. D (1985) 'The balance thesis – contextual effects of ability on pupils' "O" grade examination results', *Oxford Review of Education*, 11(1): 33–41.

Woodhead, C. (1998) 'What makes a good teacher', *Parliamentary Brief*, 5(7): 31.

11 Policy and governance

John Tomlinson

Integrity in its dual senses of wholeness and moral uprightness is the informing principle of education. It is the objective desired and pursued for each pupil; it is required of teachers individually and collectively in their transactions with children, colleagues and parents; and integrity must inform the learning processes and structures of the school. To the extent that this is achieved, the school can become a moral community, that is a community in which all are valued, all can give service and all can grow. Individual identity, in its diversities of expression, is fostered, but within a matrix of fraternity: independence understanding its need for interdependence.

How far do current interpretations of education and structures for schooling identify and support this kind of integrity and to the extent that they do not, what could be done?

The social and political context

The radical re-structuring of the maintained schools system since the late 1970s has given us several different models of the school and its purpose. For example:

(a) *The competitive, market model* construes the school as a business enterprise, competing for pupils and hence resources. Parents, acting as proxy consumers on behalf of their children, are given market information such as 'league tables', school prospectuses, governors' annual reports and inspection reports to assist them in making choices. Sanctions include complaints procedures and the 'right' to move the child to another school.

(b) *The dual-empowerment model* construes the school as an enterprise in which there are both internal and external stakeholders. The alleged professional monopoly of power has been broken by bringing parents, business-people and community figures into both the government and management. It is based on a political idea about the redistribution of power. At the same time,

(c) *The managerial model* has devolved responsibility for finance, staffing and management to school level, following the 'efficiency of devolution' theory.

(d) *The quality control model* construes the school as the engine by which certain public requirements are delivered. Hence the national curriculum, pupil testing and assessment, budgetary control and teacher appraisal are required externally, realised in the school, and then judged externally by inspection, testing and examination results. The teachers are workers in someone else's factory, making someone else's products.

It may be observed that schools are expected to operate all four models simultaneously. Yet the value systems they represent and require for their success are very different, and in some respects contradictory, even incompatible. Schools have always pursued many purposes and teachers have carried many roles, but the contemporary political construction of schooling has imposed particular stresses – a built-in cognitive dissonance. For example, success in the market place may not be seen as compatible with retaining pupils who need special attention, and the increase in school exclusions is evidence of this. Cooperative planning within a school does not sit easily with parents and senior staff seen as critics rather than colleagues, or departmental rivalry for the resources to achieve better examination results.

These observations are raised at this point because any account of, or exhortation about, school policy and governance cannot avoid taking a view of them – unless it is to be dismissed by practitioners as out of touch with reality. Every governing body, head and school staff has to create a context in which these tensions are acknowledged and held under control. To the extent that this is avoided or fudged, the school is dysfunctional. Moreover, the resulting ethos constitutes the school's most significant long-term effect on children. Good school government involves finding ways to create processes that are laden with the values desired. It is an unavoidable aspect of the necessary complexity of education, which is another central theme of this book.

It seems unlikely that the controversies over the deeper purposes of education, which have given these complexities such salience in the last twenty years, will be removed by the policies proposed for the next few years. The question to what extent the school should be an autonomous, isolated, self-interested body, or, instead, part of a cooperative public service will not be resolved quickly, after the radical changes so recently imposed. Compare two public statements:

> no governing body has the right to affect the fortunes of another school without a proper public process.
> (Walter Ulrich, National Association of Governors and Managers, reported in the *Times Educational Supplement*, 5 July 1996)

Grant maintained schools must have the right to

> make their own decisions about how they operate and what sort of schools they want to be . . . [and so to] develop the character they judge will best suit the needs of their pupils and their communities without being told by anyone else what to do.
> (Gillian Shephard, Secretary of State for Education, 28 March 1996)

> There is no reconciling these viewpoints. The first sees the schools as part of a common public effort; the second sees the public interest as achieved by a multiplicity of individual institution-interested decisions.

The process of vastly increasing the powers of central government while transferring responsibility from the LEAs to governing bodies competing amongst themselves

> is replacing political control by [local] elected bodies with a responsibility for providing education for a whole population with quasi-autonomous schools which manage their budgets, shape their image, and [increasingly] select their intakes. This is claimed to de-politicise education. It does not. It embodies a different politics. Decisions not taken by central government are transferred from the public sphere and made into largely 'private' matters.
> (Edwards 1997: 20)

Current policy proposes to retain schools of differing status, is unclear about sensible and fair admission arrangements and suggests local ballots about selection (with the almost certain effect of reinforcing differentiation of schools). Most importantly, for the theme of this chapter, it continues to conceive of education as being primarily the province of atomised, isolated schools. The Education Action Zone may prove to be an alternative to this philosophy; yet it is not advocated for that reason but to save failing schools.

However, it is clear that many schools and local authorities have reacted against this conceptualisation, even during the period of its most assertive hegemony. There is ample evidence to suggest that many schools, LEAs and university departments of education have formed partnerships and networks of mutual support for initial teacher training, induction of newly qualified teachers, and continuing professional development for more senior staff, including Heads (Ranson and Tomlinson 1994; Bines and Welton 1995; Bridges and Husbands 1996).

Bridges and Husbands, for example, illustrate

> one of the somewhat paradoxical consequences of the development of the education market place: the development of collaborative relations and infrastructures between what are in significant respects competing institutions. In some cases these have taken the form of relatively loose networks linking individuals . . . in others more formally defined and structured consortia of institutions.

The authors conclude that those involved in these innovations, 'continue to find meaning and motivation in notions of community, collegiality and collaboration' (Bridges and Husbands 1996: 2–6).

It seems most likely that the next few years, as the policies of the government evolve, will see the working out of a re-moulded matrix of inter-dependencies within the schools system, including the LEAs and higher education. At their best, some of these collaborations will be the kind of '*transformative partnerships* in which the participants actively and critically shape joint endeavours to improve all facets of education' (Graham 1997). Indeed, 'partnership' is a word used ubiquitously in the White Paper *Excellence in Schools* (1997), and it may yet prove to be the stronger force unleashed by the new government. It would certainly sit more comfortably with the post-school policies for *lifelong learning* and *the learning society* so stridently advocated and in such contrast to the tight control of learning pressed upon the schools.

What might 'good governance', in the school and beyond, look like? It would be a lively compound of public accountability and professional responsibility.

- It would require of government a willingness to set only broad objectives, leaving the teachers to devise the processes (thereby writing the unique signature of each school), public inspection to judge the quality of both process and achievement, and the profession itself, acting as a consciously responsible collective, to set standards of training and professional practice, subject only to what the public was willing to afford.

- In the localities it would require lay persons with adequate time to offer and an understanding of education and its complexities to take part in both school governance and city/county/regional bodies, so as to balance the interests of the individual school within the wider public interest in the distribution of pupils, staff and other resources, and to encourage the interplay of schools, universities, social and health services and the economic life of the area. Such lay persons would themselves need to be accountable, whether by election or otherwise.
- It would require of teachers that they learned the hard lessons of peer review and how it meshed with external inspection and quality assurance procedures to improve school processes and offer public satisfaction. It would require that teachers nationally, through the General Teaching Council, should promulgate and police a code of professional practice in publicly visible ways, and with appropriate appeals procedures.

There can be no pretence that such a system, if it could be established, would be so much in equilibrium as to remain stable, in the face of social and political buffeting over time. How might its resilience be ensured? The history of public education in England in the twentieth century suggests a cycle which permitted extremes. In its latest phase a perceived excess of teacher and school autonomy has led to an exceptional degree of central control affecting all aspects of the service – curriculum, examinations, training and inspection. In the past, militancy has been seen by teachers as their only weapon against oppressive control, whether pedagogical or administrative. The question for the future is what might be the alternative to militancy? The answer on offer is increased autonomy for the school, which places in the hands of teachers opportunities to exercise control over organisation and priorities formerly exercised from outside, and, at the national level, the General Teaching Council through which teachers will have a direct effect on standards of entry to the profession, further professional training and professional conduct. The Register of those entitled to teach will, for the first time, be maintained by the profession itself.

The task will be to make of these new mechanisms the proper balance between external accountability (the national curriculum, standards of training and inspection) and professional responsibility (peer review, appraisal, and a professional code of conduct).

Given that these circumstances will be only emergent in the period concerning this text, those responsible for schools must find their way among slippery policies and make up their own minds about the fundamental values they wish to model to the pupils and to the community. This will be true for the school, LEA, Education Action Zone and for any other device that may be introduced. That is no bad thing: it offers some opening for originality in an otherwise over-controlled system and thus reveals the gateways to that better, more balanced, future. But it needs imagination and courage.

Policy and governance – inside the school

What sense can be made of the first interpretation of *integrity* offered in this text, namely, *integrity as wholeness*? The starting point is to ask what is the most important purpose of a school. It must be to help its pupils *learn*. Once learning is accepted as the informing principle of the organisation, a host of cognate questions and challenges arise and need their answers embodying in the over-arching policies of the school. *How* do people learn? *What* are they to learn?

The elements of learning

Learning is both a private and a social activity. This is true of both the cognitive and the affective domains. To understand the power of those apparently simple statements, and to make the attempt to create an array of learning processes and settings which might make learning truly accessible to the variety of mind and personality encountered every day in school, constitutes an endeavour worthy of any professional teacher – and one which enjoins humility as much as intelligence.

A good learning environment involves a compound of the following elements which raise the questions: How does each pupil learn best? What should be the learning goals? What is distinctive about the knowledge to be learned? What will constitute evidence of learning? And, how shall we assess?

(a) Understanding how the pupil learns best. From the earliest stages and throughout life, learning is achieved through combinations of the senses providing data which both form and inform the mind. The mind does not merely receive 'input' but works to make sense of it and thereby extends its own capacity. To understand and assist in this mysterious process going on within each child is the first duty of the teacher. In the jargon, it will provide clues about appropriate teaching techniques and settings – the pedagogy.

(b) The next question is what should be the learning goals. The arrival of a national curriculum has, in the popular mind – and perhaps in the mind of some politicians and national educational bodies – removed the necessity for this question. The fact that this is so far removed from the truth is a clue to one of the underlying pathologies of education at the moment. To have named the 'subject matter' to be learned is only the beginning, and the easiest part. Faced with the range of mind, personality, motivation, linguistic ability and social experience of a classroom of children the teacher has to choose and operate a variety of detailed learning experiences calculated to engage each child according to the nature of his or her learning. Thus do curriculum and pedagogy merge and interact.

(c) Each 'subject' has its own ways of investigating the world, its own language of discourse, and its own tests for truth. That is the defining nature of what we have come to call 'subjects'. Each represents a different way humankind has discovered to investigate the worlds around us and within us. To 'do', say, mathematics, is importantly different from 'doing' history, fine art or engineering. All too often, the so-called learning is left at the superficial level of 'facts', whereas the real importance of each subject lies in coming to understand those inner structures and processes which give it its special nature – and the mastery of which gives the student the ability to become one who can begin to learn for him or herself. This is perhaps the most neglected aspect of teaching, even in universities. But it is the most fundamental. It is as true in the teaching of the very young as it is in secondary schools, or further and higher education. And it relates to knowledge, understanding and skills in many fields, not just the most 'cerebral' aspects of learning. In providing for balance, progression and coherence in the curriculum, as experienced by the learner over a term or a year, teachers also need to have regard to 'areas of experience', a meta-level of analysis of subject-matter in which the skills and understandings which separate subjects have in common are teased out. The connection and development of these across the curriculum can then be planned for and monitored (e.g. Department for Education and Science 1983).

(d) It is necessary to decide what will constitute evidence of learning, as the process itself continues. This is importantly different from the terminal assessment at the end of a module, term, year or other punctuation point. Assessment *in* and *from* learning allows both teacher and learner to tell whether the methods and content chosen are having the results intended. It creates continuing feedback and allows teacher and student to collaborate in an unthreatening relationship to improve the process and content of learning, should that be necessary. Watch any infants teacher going round a busy class, or listen to a seminar leader with a group of lively undergraduates. It is part of the professionalism at any stage.

(e) Lastly, it will be necessary to prepare the pupil or student for the form in which the final assessment will be made. Each form of test, laboratory report, record of activity or examination has its own language, format and style. It is the task of the teacher to ensure that the pupil is familiar and confident with them.

What is to be learned?

What is to be learned, through the processes just described? A school which has created its own life – integrity – has learned how to 'deliver' what is required by public ordinance, the national curriculum, religious education, health education etc., and has added its own unique signature by reflecting, with the local community, upon what the demands and expectations of parents, employers, community leaders and most of all, the pupils themselves mean for growing up successfully in their particular context. Integrity as wholeness means the melding of all these elements of curriculum and styles of learning into an education dynamic with its own impetus, in which the elements inform and reinforce one another, rather than being held apart. In this way learning acquires increasing coherence as received by the pupil over time, instead of the subjects and understandings being left hanging and unconnected.

Structures and values

The cement which holds such a school together is its value system. A school must be a moral community if it is to be anything. That means continually exploring the ethics of the common life. Thus may be approached the goal posed earlier, a community in which all can share, all are valued, and all are expected to give service. Note, *not* a community in which all are expected to do the same or become the same. Good education is about the cultivation of unique individual identity, the maximum of desirable individual differences, but within a matrix of fraternity. In such a milieu each child can be helped to the realisation that others must also feel, as he or she does, a sense of self awareness and personal worth; and that, therefore they must be accorded the same respect and opportunities. Such a school is a microcosm of the pluralistic society and offers an ordered structure within which the mixtures of the individual and communal values required for social cohesion can first be directly experienced and learned for future family life and citizenship.

The best schools have amply demonstrated that the education service contains the wisdom needed to realise this kind of social and educational milieu. The objective is a school that is alive, self-critical and self-developing, in touch with pupils, parents and the wider community. Such a school has learned the true meaning of accountability. The uses made of the word 'accountability' over the last decade or so might suggest its root is 'accountancy'. It is not. The root is 'account', that is, a story. Good accountability lies in a truthful understanding of the school's inner life and the ability to tell that story – to those inside and those outside. The capacity to tell your story, whether as a person or a group, is a fundamental mark of humanity. We are the heirs to the countless conversations of humankind since primeval times and it is through those that we have defined ourselves and our world, and given our lives meaning and purpose. Schools likewise that would be effective at the deepest levels need to build the vocabulary and occasions of that inner dialogue which constructs and expresses their moral world. Only within such a context may truthful understandings be exchanged of why children have learned – or not learned. It is striking to a perceptive visitor that some schools have created an individual language for this inner dialogue, while others have not, and are thus still trapped in the vocabulary and hence the concepts pressed upon them by external agencies such as SCAA/QCA or OFSTED. The first have insight; the others only technical knowledge.

Schools of this self-developing, open nature know what they are attempting to do, how they will do it, the tests for success and the evidence that will be collected on the way. They know who is responsible for each aspect and are able to use the findings as positive feedback to improve the next attempts or inform new purposes. Such a way of working does not hold 'staff development', 'curriculum development' and 'organisational development' apart as separate activities (as is done so often), but relates them so that they work hand-in-hand to contribute to the continual burnishing of the whole concept of the school: integrity as wholeness.

In the collegial school thus described each teacher will feel an individual clarity of purpose and identity with the processes of accountability. In addition, there will be a collective framework of purpose and judgement shared with colleagues and visible to all working at the school and to the wider community of governors, parents and public. Legitimation of the roles of both governors and professionals springs from this soil. The impetus to improvement is rooted in the conscientiousness of both the individual and the collective, not in authoritarianism.

The curriculum in such a school holds three aspects paramount.

1 The personal and social development of all the pupils. Unless they are 'growing up', emotionally as well as physically and intellectually, children cannot make the best of what is offered, no matter how well it may be taught.

2 A range of learning systems – teaching methods, pupil organisation and curriculum materials – that gives *all* the opportunity to learn, in different but equally valued ways.

3 Attention to the hidden curriculum. That is to say, the invisible web of values that informs every act and structure of the school, whether intended or not. Living it, not merely talking it. Children see through phoney adults mercilessly – remember Holden Caulfield in *The Catcher in the Rye*? They only respect and learn from those who are sincere.

Two interpretations of integrity are considered in this book: integrity as wholeness and integrity as truthfulness or uprightness. It will now be clear how central both of them are to the good school. Policy and governance must focus on wholeness because however good the parts (individual teachers or departments) what the pupil experiences is also, and perhaps predominantly, the total effect of the school's ethos. And truthfulness is at the heart of processes of teaching and review. There may be fine quality assurance systems on paper, but unless they are carried out with integrity they are without value or effect. Or rather, at the extreme, their effect can be malign because their neglect creates a culture of evasion. A school which acts out a sham becomes corrupt.

Increased complexity – the world beyond the school

It will now be clear how necessarily complex are the processes essential within a good school. It has always been a feature of teaching that teachers carry many roles simultaneously, shift between them autonomously as occasion demands (rather than waiting for an instruction), and that the children understand the valences of these differing roles and react accordingly. Consultants from the world of business, where tasks tend to be more singularly defined and line management accountabilities more emphasised, often remark on this feature of schools.

To this 'internal' complexity must now be added other dimensions, because schools live an anything but hermetic existence. To the contrary,

- children learn increasingly through extra-school processes such as the TV and information technology in home and community;
- children also inhabit other moral worlds of family, street, popular culture, and peer group. Through these they encounter alternative and often conflicting value systems; and
- as we have noted, schools serve societal and political ends and have to accept content and values imposed from outside.

In this context, the relationship between the teaching profession collectively and the political nation assumes crucial significance. After thirty years – a generation of adults and six of schoolchildren – of a growing central grip on the detail of education there is still disquiet about educational performance, yet further prescription of curriculum (literacy and numeracy hours) and, currently, proposals for 'a major restructuring of the profession' (Department for Education and Employment 1999). It is becoming clear to many that part of the problem may be that we have no means by which the profession or the public can ask serious questions or raise issues and hope to get well-informed discussion which might lead to change if enough of us wanted it. As the Editors ask in their Introduction, 'In what public domain are the models of acceptable performance thrashed out and agreed?' Put in terms of the health of our civil society, the question is, 'Where is the democratic space in which discussion of educational policy can take place and have its legitimate effect upon the governors?'

All the instruments and organisations of the so-called period of consensus from the 1940s to the 1970s have been demolished as representing and supporting a corporatist and middle-of-the-road approach which at the same time would be both too frail and too cumbersome to serve the need for sharp and rapid responses to cope with global competition and never-ending change. In such a climate, when government or one of its agencies issues consultation documents the outcome is virtually foreclosed. Consultation and comment are confined to the agenda and proposals being put forward. The earlier stage, of asking what we want to achieve and reviewing options for doing it, has either been set aside in favour of a dogma or taken place behind closed doors. This in turn creates a situation where those who may suggest alternatives are characterised as being against the objectives, when it is the process they would have different. In the polarisation that follows relations are soured and less is achieved than might have been.

There are serious reasons for thinking that the education of our children has become over-prescribed and the schools too enmeshed in the language and mentality of targets, inspection and league tables. The deficit model of how to cause improvement ('failing schools', 'name and shame') is not the only one available. Nor is it the model most favoured in many other fields of successful enterprise, where building on strengths and a 'can-do' approach has been proved to work – especially where the independent commitment of the practitioner is crucial to the quality of the outcome. Those who think thus are not arguing against high standards and vibrant schools. Quite the contrary. But they are concerned at the growing evidence of a dysfunctional anxiety among pupils, teachers – and many parents. The structural problem for our society is that this anxiety remains free-floating because there is no accepted way in which it can be rationally examined, and either be shown to be groundless or, if it is not, lead to changes that will improve the lives of children.

The seeds of a more open educational society may just be discernible in some of the policies of government. They need more nurture. And government should declare now that its aim is to move from the existing 'high control/low trust' regime to less control and more trust in the profession, provided declared milestones of improvement are reached along the road.

A less prescriptive National Curriculum from 2000, underpinned by a real belief in personal/social education, the proposals for the career-long professional development of teachers and the freedoms offered in Educational Action Zones may be the harbingers of a better climate. Most crucially, the creation of a General Teaching Council, which was due to open in September 2000, offers the opportunity of creating what I have called democratic space. The profession has waited for more than a century for a government with the courage to legislate a GTC. The Council and the profession will carry a grave responsibility to behave responsibly if the opportunities are not to be squandered.

The legitimacy of the General Teaching Council will arise from its being a body which uniquely brings together those who provide education and those who use it. The whole profession (Further and Higher Education will be represented, though the focus is on schoolteachers), will sit with governors, LEAs, churches, parents, employers and other public interests to advise on the best ways to train and develop teachers, to estimate the numbers that will be needed in the future, and to declare and monitor the standards and conduct required of the profession. It is an opportunity to re-learn some of the political wisdom of the age of consensus. Since some of those who would later have to take political decisions will be involved in the Council's deliberations, it should be clear to its members what are the parameters of the politically possible. Such a mature approach would make all the more telling those few occasions when a difference of view with the government of the day had to be declared.

In Scotland there has been a GTC since 1966. In 1992–3 the Scottish Office undertook a policy review of the GTC. Its conclusions in relation to the advice on teacher supply are relevant to the prospect for England:

> the close match between the qualifications of Scottish teachers and the subjects they are required to teach stands in sharp contrast to the position in England and Wales where there is no equivalent of the General Teaching Council. This impressive correlation between qualifications held and tuition given is due in no small part to the Council's influence. It must be recognised that, were there no such body, the retention of this level of control would be extremely difficult and standards in Scottish education would be at risk.
>
> (Scottish Office Education Department 1992: 3)

Here is control which is both effective and accepted because it was devised co-operatively and serves ends all support. The Report continues:

> any developments proposed are discussed in a collaborative environment and are likely to receive a more positive reception than would be the case were a Government department seeking to impose top-down changes.

Such an approach is possible in England with regard not only to the supply of teachers but also to the entry standards required of teachers, the curriculum of initial teacher training, the induction of new teachers and the continuing professional development of all teachers. It is, literally, a millennial opportunity. Teachers and their collaborators will need to show they can rise to it; government will need to be mature enough to work with it.

Conclusions

The agenda adumbrated here for the good school and the good educational polity requires holding in creative tension the immediate and the transcendental. Schools are society's servants and must do its bidding. But teachers are the educated and privileged heirs to a humane tradition which through religious texts, philosophy, poetry, music, drama and literature has shown us in successive generations how we may become more human. It has set inexorably before us the vision that nobility of soul is possible, or, at least, decency. It is the task of the teacher to realise this anew with each new generation. It means working at a precept offered long ago: 'Render unto Caesar the things that are Caesar's, and unto God the things that are God's.'

If this is accepted as the schools' part in rearing the young, then it must follow that the task of the intermediate and mediating bodies is directly to support them. The task of government must be to set the wider parameters and to provide the national inspiration and the sinews of resources.

There is an enduring 'curriculum for humanity' which is the leitmotif of education, and which must be pursued beyond the instrumental curriculum demanded by any particular culture in any particular period. The work of humanisation has a fundamental and unchanging character. But it must be melded with the demands of the day and actualised in a thousand ways and settings, as it has been through time. That is the work of education: 'Education is simply the soul of a society as it passes from one generation to another' (G. K. Chesterton).

References

Bines, H. and Welton, J. (1995) *Managing Partnerships in Teacher Training and Development*, London: Routledge.

Bridges, D. and Husbands, C. (1996) *Consorting and Collaborating in the Educational Marketplace*, London: Falmer Press.

Department for Education and Employment (1999) *Performance Management Framework for Teachers: Consultation Document*, London: DfEE.

Department for Education and Science (1983) *Curriculum 11–16: Towards a Statement of Entitlement*, London: HMSO.

Edwards, A. (1997) 'Consumer rights and common purposes' in P. Mortimore and V. Little (eds), *Living Education – Essays in Honour of John Tomlinson*, London: Paul Chapman.

Graham, J. (1997) 'Partnerships in Education', Unpublished paper given at University of East London.

Ranson, S. and Tomlinson, J. (1994) *School Co-operation: New Forms of Local Governance*, Harlow: Longman.

Scottish Office Education Department (1992) *GTC for Scotland: Policy Review 1992–93*, Edinburgh: Scottish Office.

12 And how will we get there from here?

Chris Watkins, Ron Best and Caroline Lodge

A concluding chapter to this volume would miss the point if it tried to be conclusive. Rather, an attempt must be made to think about the next steps of the continuing journey, and about what will be needed to create our preferred futures. The foregoing chapters carry some strong messages on this score. Each contributor was asked to 'take an idea for a walk' in their writing, and some important themes emerge from the different journeys they have taken for themselves and on which they have invited you to join them. Two are highlighted here.

1   *Seeing connectedness.* Whether it is in how we understand a school, how we think about a curriculum or learning landscape, or how we make sense of children, young people, or their teachers, there has been a strong stance towards seeing connections between parts. No matter what the complexity of the various elements, the wish to recognise and 'see' the connections has been a feature of these authors' perspectives. As a way of seeing, this stance contrasts with those who see the parts in ever smaller scale and in the process pay little heed to what binds them together. The latter, atomistic approach is associated with the creation of lists: pupils as lists of achievements, curricula as lists of knowledge, teachers as lists of competences, organisations as lists of people and duties. This cannot be a complete picture and cannot therefore be a picture which has the first quality of integrity which we seek, that of wholeness. This word is not meant to imply that there is a particular or fixed whole to be seen and that this is of value in itself. The stance of seeing connections and wholes creates a richer and more complete picture than would otherwise be the case. Additionally, it leads to enhanced achievement of what is important: which links to our second theme.

2   *Valuing connectedness.* Again, whether we talk about the relations between schools and their communities, between various
parts of a learning offer, or between adults and children in a learning context, the authors in this volume have demonstrated the
value which derives from attending to, nurturing and prioritising
such relations. In various ways, attention which is given to promoting the whole through nourishing the connections leads to an
improved state of affairs – as indicated by terms in our language
such as 'wholesome' and 'healthy' which come from the same
root – the middle English 'hale' as in 'hale and hearty'. Again the
whole health of an individual, group or organisation is not being
propounded in a particular or fixed way, but in a way which can
embrace diversity. This is also where the valuing of connectedness
relates to the valuing of complexity. A modern view of integrity is
not to be confused with a static view of moral uprightness: this
could be fundamentalism. Notions of change and development
must be incorporated so that our individual, organisational and
societal futures develop towards increased complexity, a goal
which education at its best has always found easy to adopt.

In the current times of judging a school by the (so over-emphasised)
performance outcomes, some may think that the considerations sum-
marised above do not fit, but in fact evidence of a range of sorts affirms
the value of this stance, even for its impact on measurable performance. For example, we know that schools with a strong sense of
community get better results in these terms (Bryk *et al.* 1993). We
know that schools with a collaborative ethos amongst teachers get
better results (Rosenholtz 1991), and we know not only that schools
with more connected practices show gains in academic performance at
least 20 per cent above those which used more divisive approaches (Lee
and Smith 1995) but also that student gains are distributed more equi-
tably. Achievement gains in these terms are greater in schools where
teachers take collective responsibility for students' academic success or
failure (Lee and Smith 1996). Further, we know that when adolescents feel
connected to their schools they are less likely to be involved in practices
harmful to their health (Resnick *et al.* 1997) and that when classrooms
are constructed in ways that emphasise a pro-social learning community
there are improvements in social dispositions, learning motivation and
metacognitive skills (Battistich *et al.* 1999) as well in levels of student
drug use and delinquency (Battistich and Hom 1997). Promoting
connectedness contributes to the common good: it is valuable for learning,
change, and a range of other positive outcomes. This second sense of

integrity highlights it as a valuable quality which is both implied and promoted by taking the whole, connected view of our interests and concerns.

Given these themes, where now? How shall we think about moving ahead? One element of our thinking must be our underlying approach to promoting change. Brighouse and Woods (1999: 146) identify three different approaches:

(a) *Problem-solving*. Here the steps are: (i) identify problems; (ii) analyse causes; (iii) analyse solutions; and (iv) develop action plans. As an approach, this can work well, but there is a clear danger of exhaustion if it is over-used. Students too become strategic in such a situation, as some 17-year-olds said to MacDonald (2000) when asked 'What do you remember most?' about careers lessons. They replied 'thousands and thousands of action plans!' and 'I know by heart what to put in them, I know exactly what they want to hear, and I know exactly what phrases to use!'

(b) *Appreciative inquiry*. This starts from a crucially different first step: (i) appreciate the best of what is; (ii) envision what might be; (iii) dialogue for new knowledge and ideas – what should be; (iv) innovate – what will be. Brighouse argued that we need to do this more, especially for future development of the education system (see also Hammond, 1996).

(c) *Ensuring compliance*. Here the steps are: (i) decide what is right; (ii) promulgate single solutions; (iii) regulate and inspect; (iv) punish in public deviants and delinquents. Teachers and others identify this as the dominant approach from government in England at the current time.

The final comment highlights an important element of the contemporary context in England and (perhaps to a lesser extent) other parts of the UK. We need to recognise the depth to which compliance has become the climate of government policy and school practice, and ask whether it will really be an appropriate approach to future change. Contributors to this volume were asked not to look backward and re-fight old educational battles on a political platform. They have achieved this and managed not to become organised by the policy position which they find wanting. In this they have demonstrated the spirit of appreciative enquiry to lift our sights to a further horizon. Notwithstanding this, it is time to think about what would be needed to step from here towards the futures we seek.

Perhaps the title of this chapter may have reminded you of a very old joke in which a person asking for directions was told 'well if I was you I wouldn't start from here'. And many teachers we meet feel a sense of 'stuckness' with the current state which the education system has reached. In the UK and in other westernised nations the course for education has been influenced by an increased role taken by politicians in deciding matters of educational policy. In the UK since 1988 legislation has paid ever-increasing attention to matters of detail on many fronts.

To understand the knowledge and action perspective of policy-makers, Watkins and Mortimore (1999) have argued that we need to recognise the new forms of monitoring and control which have been pursued through government agencies, their formal inspection frameworks and models of teacher competence. Policy-makers simplify matters such as pedagogy in order to shape their new role. In so doing they appear to have reverted to a nineteenth-century view of the 'object lesson' – a set piece deemed to have universal application. This is where tensions arise with the knowledge bases of teacher practitioners and of academic researchers, together with their associated views of action.

A changed set of relations between teachers, academics and policy makers has emerged (see Figure 12.1). Practitioners are treated as functionaries and the stance of policy-makers towards them is one of a 'hostile witness'. By the same token researchers have been accused of acting like 'collusive lovers' towards the teaching force. Understanding

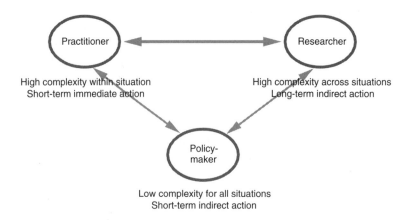

Figure 12.1 Practitioner, researcher and policy-maker knowledge.

these current relations makes it more possible to take a distance on them. Teachers may be helped to understand that their voice is not the same as that of policy-makers, and this is a crucial part of re-professionalising and re-asserting their voice in the new context.

In today's schools we see a range of responses from teachers to the challenges of the current context, especially the increased pressures. We characterise these as:

1 Cave in – lower expectations, relax demands, dumb-down the curriculum (end result: teacher disengagement).

2 Pass it on – more sanctions, more worksheets, more tests (end result: teacher burnout and cynicism).

3 Wise up – teach for understanding, build learning communities (end result: teacher sense of efficacy, but doubtless with ongoing frustration).

In tomorrow's schools we need to create the conditions where teachers are supported and challenged to re-professionalise and learn – about the changing context, about their particular context and about the processes of learning. Undoubtedly public pressures will persist, but learning is a large part of the answer to how to respond to those pressures in a proactive way. The most recent evidence on UK secondary schools (Gray *et al.* 1999) confirms that the most improving schools have shifted beyond tactics and strategies into an area which builds its capacity to improve, through an overarching focus on learning. Such a shift may involve:

• Organisational learning, through which each school ensures the health of its own processes, and also goes beyond the cycle of comparing its performance with operating targets to question whether its operating targets are appropriate.

• Group learning, in which the processes of building learning communities are exercised for teachers as well as for students.

• Individual learning, including the increasingly important capacity of learning about one's own learning.

Part of what will be required of teachers and schools in the future, and is required of them now in order to get there, is a perspective which sees connections in order to compose a whole picture, and which also supports the active questioning and challenging of any policy and practice which does not promote connectedness. Integrity has to be fought for. In our own professional experience we, the editors of this volume, find that such a perspective is aided by identifying the forms of talk which do and those which do not support that cause.

The various ways in which learning, schooling and so on are talked about have various effects, some of them planned and some unwitting. Through different discourses, different versions of a topic may be created. 'A discourse refers to a set of meanings, metaphors, representations, images, stories and so on that in some way produce a particular version of events' (Burr, 1995: 48). For example Ball (1993, 1994) has identified a 'discourse of derision' in the comments of politicians and press, through which ideas of complexity are rubbished and their sources are vilified without intellectual argument. At the same time a *discourse of deficit and failure* has been widespread, in which the predominant talk is focused on what is *not* deemed to be occurring in schools, rather than what is. This is usually associated with a critical or negative judgement, so it has a general impact of finding schools and teachers wanting in our society. The supposed solution constructs another discourse of its own, *the discourse of 'standards'*, which soon gets confused with standardisation, places great emphasis on tests (which seldom measure what matters and have limited potential for the reforms which are really needed) and tends to put at risk the communal processes of trust. It creates an inevitable narrowing and distortion of the purposes and achievements of schools, and hi-jacks the core human purposes in education. Using testing as a means of teacher surveillance and blame reduces its potential for promoting learning. Surveillance does not provide the conditions for teachers to take active responsibility for their learning.

Each of the above discourses opposes the tomorrow which is emerging, as does that mentioned already – the *discourse of compliance*. It arises as a result of the increased detail of government policies and a 'one-size-fits-all' style. At the end of the twentieth century, when it became increasingly clear that national governments have little impact on international economics, they turn their attention to domestic matters and do so with a legislative/mechanical turn of mind which is manifested in many policy-making processes. The impact on many teachers has been to create a 'what do we have to do now?' approach to educational reform, which of course is inimical to real change. Some recognition of this dynamic is available in the public domain, for example when our current breed of politicians is referred to as 'control freaks' and so on. But it is clear that schools do not improve through compliance. Rosenholtz's (1991) study of seventy-eight schools gave evidence of many differences between 'moving schools' and 'stuck schools'. When teachers were asked the question: 'Do you ever have to do things that are against the rules in order to do what's best for your students?', 79 per cent of those in moving schools answered 'Yes', while 75 per cent of those in stuck schools answered 'No'.

Taken together, the combined impact of the above discourses is negative and backward-looking: they promote, perhaps unintentionally, a factory model of schooling at just the time when we should be transcending it. They do not promote an open examination of what developments and dialogues a twenty-first century schooling system should incorporate. Their impact on public thinking should not be under-estimated, but at the same time we do not hesitate to say that they are wrong-headed and inadequate. Alternatives are needed and, as this volume has shown, are available. The evidence is also beginning to show that the above discourses have a divisive impact on the achievements of young people in our schools, with signs of polarisation in the population at many points of performance.

It is not new to propose that looking towards the future demands of us a new way of thinking and talking. Drucker (1990, cited in Beare, 1996) proposed that by the 1980s

> we passed out of the creeds, commitments and alignments that had shaped the politics for a century or two. . . . There is now a 'new world view', and it is best demonstrated by a fundamental change in the imagery we use to describe the world and human activity. We have moved from using mechanical or mechanistic metaphors to explain how the world and people work, to biological metaphors – from machines to living systems.

Our education system seems to be having some difficulty in making the move which Drucker describes.

More appropriate to the processes and purposes of education is a *discourse of honouring*: honouring and supporting the richness of people's experiences, the complexity of their life-knowledges and so on, for both pupils and teachers. In this way schools might become communities of acknowledgement (McLean 1995) rather than of critical judgement, and through this process greater engagement would ensue. Our faith in that result is supported by our perspective on learning processes, on human beings, and on their interactions: it is this discourse which currently needs understanding, enhancement and becoming more practised. Such a perspective brings focus to the unique and remarkable characteristics of our being human, and recognition of the complexity and creativity of human purpose. It demands an enhanced *discourse of human agency*. This is also a discourse which is not dominant in today's schools but which must be more so in tomorrow's: how it may be nurtured and developed by an education system is worthy of investment and experiment. For it relates to the key connecting *discourse of interaction, construction and learning.* Here our ways of describing the growth of meaning and the processes of development need strengthening. Then our helping young people construct a valid and pro-social purpose to their lives, both in school and beyond, may truly support them in composing a life (in contrast with the old conceptions of 'deciding' or 'determining' or 'choosing' or 'preparing for' a life). Such a perspective not only supports flexibility for a world of change, it also honours the diversity, plurality, and complexity which many twentieth century perspectives have found hard to accommodate.

The need to think systemically and plurally is strong, and also to fight the notion that this is 'mindless happy talk'. Perhaps this point is best made by Finn, an 11-year-old boy, who has been surrendered by families on twenty-two occasions, and who seems clear that the mechanical discourse is inappropriate and thin. He writes about people who have worked with him: 'They talk about strengths and weaknesses but strengths are always the things we need to get more of and weaknesses are what we've already got' (Perry 1999: 65). He probably knows well how tough it is to compose a life of integrity in a context of change and possible fragmentation.

To summarise, we see the need for a changed world view, and a different way of talking. We also recognise that we have a way to go. As we begin to identify the openings of a path, we know that the steps may not always be easy, and they demand of us the human qualities which also inhabit the improved discourses we have briefly mentioned above. Human qualities of integrity are in demand, in its sense of being upright, something which others may refer to as being brave. Looking towards the future helps to promote such a feat; standing tall and looking towards a further horizon helps the human being be upright. Of course the potential for fragmentation and conflict re-appears if we all try to do this alone, so the need to construct futures, explore ideas and construct new dialogues and discourses reflects the need to do it together with others.

We take the view that connecting more explicitly to considerations of the future supports the process of collaboration and co-construction which builds learning communities. It also builds resilience to the forces which would divert us or would reduce our life-composing processes. At individual, group and organisational levels, we and our communities need to be proactive against the destructive forces in our environment. With such resilience we also build that quality which is key to embracing the future – hope. It derives from a belief that we can have an impact, that we can make a difference, and that we best do it together, and contrasts with the mean-spirited beliefs which underlie much current education policy. A spirit of generosity is a crucial element in re-building trust.

It never has been and never will be easy to avoid the power of established metaphors and discourses which have become conventional wisdom. For us, what feels like an ongoing struggle to improve education is helped by knowing that we need to embrace risk, knowing that no one has the full answer, and being prepared to stand up for difference in the face of pressures towards compliance. We have been helped by the belief that 'the facts are friendly', i.e. that the evidence on connectedness, collaboration, and community really does support a new view of integrity. In a situation where we feel increasingly aware of flux in our education system, yet at the same time recognise that yesterday's solutions generally maintain the intractability of improving schooling (Sarason 1990), we gain energy by thinking about the future.

In the set of connections which comprise this volume we hope to have made important connections with you and with possible futures which would secure a creative place for tomorrow's schools.

References

Ball, S. J. (1993) 'Education policy, power relations and teachers' work', *British Journal of Educational Studies*, 41(2): 106–21.
Ball, S. J. (1994) *Education Reform: a Critical and Post-structural Approach*, Buckingham: Open University Press.
Battistich, V. and Hom, A. (1997) 'The relationship between students' sense of their school as a community and their involvement in problem behaviors', *American Journal of Public Health*, 87(12): 1997–2001.
Battistich, V., Watson, M., Solomon, D., Lewis, C. and Schaps, E. (1999) 'Beyond the three R's: A broader agenda for school reform', *Elementary School Journal*, 99(5): 415–32.
Beare, H. (1996) *Education for the Third Millennium: Planning for School Futures in the Context of Global Developments*, Jolimont, Victoria: IARTV.
Brighouse, T. and Woods, D. (1999) *How to Improve Your School*, London: Routledge.
Bryk, A. S., Lee, V. E. and Holland, P. B. (1993) *Catholic Schools and the Common Good*, Cambridge MA: Harvard University Press.
Burr, V. (1995) *An Introduction to Social Constructionism*, London: Routledge.
Drucker, P. F. (1990) *The New Realities: in Government and Politics . . . in Economy and Business . . . in Society . . . and in World View*, London: Mandarin.

Gray, J., Hopkins, D., Reynolds, D., Wilcox, B., Farrell, S. and Jesson, D. (1999) *Improving Schools: Performance and Potential*, Buckingham: Open University Press.

Hammond, S. A. (1996) *The Thin Book of Appreciative Inquiry*, London: BT Press.

Lee, V. E. and Smith, J. B. (1995) 'Effects of high-school restructuring and size on early gains in achievement and engagement', *Sociology of Education*, 68(4): 241–70.

Lee, V. E. and Smith, J. B. (1996) 'Collective responsibility for learning and its effects on gains in achievement for early secondary school students', *American Journal of Education*, 104(2): 103–47.

MacDonald, J. (2000) 'Student views on careers education and guidance – what sort of feedback to Careers Co-ordinators?' in S. Askew (ed.) *Feedback for Learning*, London: Routledge

McLean, C. (1995) 'Schools as communities of acknowledgement: a conversation with Michael White', *Dulwich Centre Newsletter*, 2 and 3: 51–66.

Perry, L. (1999) 'There's a garden – somewhere' in A. Morgan (ed.) *Once Upon a Time: Narrative Therapy with Children and their Families*, Adelaide: Dulwich Centre Publications.

Resnick, M. D., Bearman, P. S., Blum, R. W., Bauman, K. E., Harris, K. M., Jones, J., Tabor, J., Beuhring, T., Sieving, R. E., Shew, M., Ireland, M., Bearinger, L. H. and Udry, J. R. (1997) 'Protecting adolescents from harm: findings from the National Longitudinal Study on Adolescent Health', *Journal of the American Medical Association*, 278(10): 823–32.

Rosenholtz, S. J. (1991) *Teachers' Workplace: the Social Organization of Schools*, New York: Teachers College Press.

Sarason, S. B. (1990) *The Predictable Failure of Educational Reform*, San Francisco: Jossey-Bass.

Watkins, C. and Mortimore, P. (1999) 'Pedagogy: what do we know?' in P. Mortimore (ed.) *Understanding Pedagogy and its Impact on Learning*, London: Paul Chapman/Sage.

Name Index

Subject Index